THE DICTIONARY OF CHARACTERS IN

Children's Literature

Beverly Ann Chin, Ph.D.
University of Montana
Former President of the National Council of Teachers of English
General Editor

Betty Carter, Ed.D.
Texas Women's University

Marilee Foglesong
Former Young Adult Coordinator, New York Public Library

Connie C. Rockman, M.L.S.
University of Bridgeport
Chair, Caldecott Award Committee

Advisers

Franklin Watts
A Division of Scholastic Inc.
New York   Toronto   London   Auckland   Sydney
Mexico City   New Delhi   Hong Kong
Danbury, Connecticut

DEVELOPED, DESIGNED, AND PRODUCED BY
BOOK BUILDERS LLC

Photographs **by permission of Harcourt, Inc.:** Illustration from THE BORROWERS, copyright 1953, 1952 by Mary Norton and renewed 1981, 1980 by Mary Norton, Beth Krush and Joe Krush, 24; Illustration from THE HUNDRED DRESSES by Eleanor Estes, illustrated by Louis Slobodkin, copyright 1944 by Harcourt Inc. and renewed 1971 by Eleanor Estes and Louis Slobodkin, 56 *bottom*. **By permission of HarperCollins Publishers:** 10, 13 *top*, 21, 26, 32, 33, 38, 40 *top*, 46, 51, 57, 61 *top*, 64. **Illustrated by Libico Maraja, courtesy of his estate:** 87. **By permission of Little, Brown and Company (Inc.):** From ARTHUR'S NOSE by Marc Brown, copyright © 1976 by Marc Brown, 16; From BEN AND ME by Robert Lawson, copyright © 1939 by Robert Lawson, copyright © renewed 1967 by John W. Boyd, 20; From LITTLE WOMEN by Louisa May Alcott, cover *top center*. **By permission of Viking Penguin, an imprint of Penguin Putnam Books for Young Readers, a division of Penguin Putnam Inc.:** From ADAM OF THE ROAD by Elizabeth Janet Gray, illustrated by Robert Lawson, copyright 1942 by Elizabeth Janet Gray and Robert Lawson, renewed © 1970 Elizabeth Janet Gray and John Boyd, Executor of the Estate of Robert Lawson, 7; From AMBER BROWN IS NOT A CRAYON by Paula Danziger, illustrated by Tony Ross, copyright © 1994 by Tony Ross, illustrations, by permission of G.P. Putnam's Sons, 12; "Puffin" Cover by Richard Egielski, copyright © 1988 by Viking Penguin Inc., from CHARLIE AND THE CHOCOLATE FACTORY by Roald Dahl, 30; From HOMER PRICE by Robert McCloskey, copyright 1943, renewed © 1971 by Robert McCloskey, 54; From LYDDIE by Katherine Paterson, jacket illustration by Debbi Chabrain, copyright © 1991 by Katherine Paterson, by permission of Lodestar Books, an affiliate of Dutton Children's books, 69; "Illustrations" by Amy Wummer, copyright © 1998 by Amy Wummer, illustrations, from MCBROOM TELLS THE TRUTH by Sid Fleischman, by permission of Price Stern & Sloan, 73; From MERLIN AND THE DRAGONS by Jane Yolen, illustrated by Li Ming, copyright © 1995 by Lightyear Entertainment, L.P., by permission of Cobblehill Books, an affiliate of Dutton Children's Books, 75; From MISS RUMPHIUS by Barbara Cooney, copyright © 1982 by Barbara Cooney Porter, 77; From MY SIDE OF THE MOUNTAIN by Jean Craighead George, copyright © 1959, renewed © 1987 by Jean Craighead George, by permission of Dutton Children's Books, 82; "Illustrations" by Louis S. Glanzman, from PIPPI LONGSTOCKING by Astrid Lindgren, translated by Florence Lamborn, copyright 1950 by the Viking Press, Inc., renewed © 1978 by Viking Penguin Inc., 89; From RABBIT HILL by Robert Lawson, copyright © 1944 by Robert Lawson, renewed copyright © 1971 by John W. Boyd, 90; From REDWALL by Brain Jacques, illustrated by Troy Howell, copyright © 1997 by Troy Howell, illustrations, by permission of Philomel Books, 92; From ROLL OF THUNDER, HEAR MY CRY by Mildred D. Taylor, Puffin cover illustration by Max Ginsburg, copyright © 1991 by Max Ginsburg, cover illustration,

(continues on page 125)

Every endeavor has been made to obtain permission to use copyrighted material. The publishers would appreciate errors or omissions being brought to their attention.

Library of Congress Cataloging-in-Publication Data

The dictionary of characters in children's literature / Beverly Ann Chin, general editor.
    p. cm.
    Includes bibliographical references and index.
    ISBN 0-531-11984-X
    1. Children's literature—Dictionaries—Juvenile literature. 2. Characters and characteristics in literature—Dictionaries—Juvenile literature. 3. Names, Personal, in literature—Dictionaries—Juvenile literature. [1. Literature—Dictionaries. 2. Characters in literature—Dictionaries.] I. Chin, Beverly Ann.

PN1008.5 .D53 2002
809′ .89282′03—dc21   2001017771

Contents

Note to the Reader

Meeting characters in literature gives you a chance to experience different kinds of adventures and emotions. Through these literary characters, you may also learn about yourself. Without leaving your chair, you can imagine how you might respond to the characters' challenges.

This dictionary contains entries that describe the characters in popular books. The entries are arranged alphabetically by book title. Using examples of the characters' words, thoughts, and actions, the entries show you how effective readers talk and write about characters. For many readers, literary characters are lifelong companions.

About Literary Awards. Many of the books discussed in this dictionary have won prizes awarded by panels of experts in the field of children's literature. These honors indicate that the work is of the highest quality. Prizes are cited at the beginning of an entry and include the Newbery Medal for the year's most distinguished contribution to literature for children (up to age 14) published in the United States; the American Library Association's Notable Children's Books; ALA's list of Best Books for Young Adults; ALA's Best of the Best; the Coretta Scott King Award for the year's outstanding children's book by an African American writer; the annual Boston Globe–Horn Book Award; the New York Times Notable Books list; and the annual National Book Award for Young People's Literature.

How to Use This Book

Each book entry in the dictionary appears in dark type in alphabetical order, not counting the word *A* or *The* at the beginning of a title. Look up both *Adam of the Road* and *The Adventures of Tom Sawyer* under *A*. After the title of the book, you will find these facts: the author, date of publication, kind of literature, and prizes. A brief discussion of plot, theme, and setting leads into information about characters in the work. Each discussion begins with the character's name in dark type.

A book title in SMALL CAPITAL LETTERS within an entry has an entry of its own at the proper alphabetical spot. At the back of the book, the Index can help you find specific characters and authors.

Note to the Educator

The entries model critical thinking for young readers who must think, talk, and write about characters in children's literature. We use the type of literary language students need to analyze characters by asking and answering questions such as: How, if at all, does a character change in the course of the work? Is this character multidimensional or narrow? What is the appeal of a character over time? How is a character similar to or different from other characters? Does the character represent a certain kind of person, or is the character a one-of-a-kind creation?

We selected characters from traditional and contemporary works as well as different cultures and times. For each entry, following a book's title, author, and date of publication, you will find the literary category: contemporary realistic fiction, historical/period fiction, fantasy/science fiction/imaginative fiction, humorous fiction, memoir, or mystery. As is often the case with classification, categories may overlap.

Accompanying some of the entries are these features: "Author's Anecdote" helps writers come alive; "From the Critics" quotes both amateurs and pros; "Other Works" lists more titles for this age group. Our purpose is to interest young readers in thinking critically about the memorable characters they meet in literature. We encourage you to use the *Dictionary* as a resource for literary conversations.

Beverly Ann Chin, *General Editor*

List of Major Characters

To find a character, look up the *title* of the book in which the character appears. (The title appears below in parentheses after the name of each character.)

Abel's Island ❖ William Steig, 1976, fantasy/science fiction/imaginative fiction, Newbery Honor Book. Abelard Hassam di Chirico Flint—a wealthy, snobbish mouse commonly known as **Abel**—is blown away in a storm and stranded alone on an island. Separated from his beloved wife, Amanda, Abel survives many hardships. In addition, he thinks about himself and his life, comes to appreciate nature, gains an understanding of others, and learns the meaning of friendship. By making sculptures of his wife and family, Abel discovers that he is an artist.

Adam of the Road ❖ Elizabeth Janet Gray, 1942, historical/period fiction, Newbery Medal. It is the year 1294 in England, and 11-year-old Adam Quartermayne—son of a wandering minstrel and a minstrel-in-training himself—is in trouble. His beloved spaniel, Nick, has been stolen, and, while looking for the dog, Adam has become separated from the person he loves most in the world—his father, Roger the Minstrel.

Adam. Adam is well-liked by all. Alone, searching the fairs and market towns for his father and his dog, Adam shows resourcefulness and courage in the face of hardship and uncertainty. At the end of his

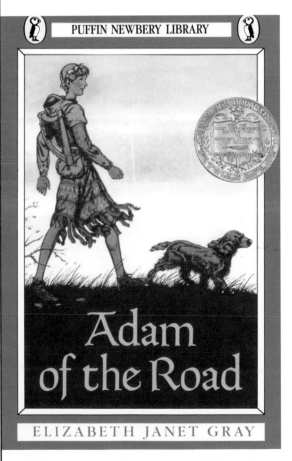

Adam is from long ago and far away but seems familiar to many readers.

wanderings, he has grown from a mischievous boy to a young man on his way to becoming a fine minstrel in his own right.

Roger. A loving father who is proud of his son, Roger feels responsible for the loss of both Adam and Nick and never gives up searching for them both.

The Adventures of Pinocchio
❖ C. Collodi, 1883, fantasy/science fiction/imaginative fiction.

Pinocchio is a marionette carved from a piece of magical talking wood by Geppetto, a puppet-maker. At first, Pinocchio is selfish and dis-

This is an illustration from an early edition of *Pinocchio*.

obedient. One of Pinocchio's problems is his habit of lying. Each time he tells a lie, his nose grows longer. Pinocchio's adventures lead him into dangerous situations. His harsh experiences and the help of Geppetto, the Talking Cricket, and the Blue Fairy gradually lead him to become a better and more honest person. As his behavior improves, Pinocchio's nose shrinks to normal size, and he comes to look more and more like a real boy.

The Adventures of Tom Sawyer
❖ Mark Twain (pen name for Samuel Langhorne Clemens), 1876, historical/period fiction. This is the story of Tom Sawyer, a young teenager growing up in a small Mississippi River town before the Civil War, and his friends.

Tom Sawyer. Tom Sawyer is one of the most famous characters in American literature. He is loyal and courageous. He stands up for his friends, risks his own life to defend an innocent man accused of murder, and faces danger in order to save his girlfriend Becky when the two are trapped in a cave. But Tom is also a mischief maker who possesses the intelligence to outwit the adults who try to keep him in line. Given the boring task of painting a fence, he so successfully convinces his friends that the job is desirable that they do it for him.

Huckleberry ("Huck") Finn. Huck Finn, the son of the town drunk, is Tom's best friend. In

Twain's autobiography, the author writes that Huck is based on a real-life friend of Twain's: "He was ignorant, unwashed, insufficiently fed: but he had as good a heart as any boy had. . . . [He] was . . . continuously happy, and was envied by all the rest of us." Huck is in the habit of doing exactly as he pleases—hunting, fishing, stealing (which Huck thinks of as "borrowing")—but does not like to go to church or school.

Aunt Polly. A kind, loving soul, Aunt Polly has her hands full with Tom, who lives with her. She loves him too much to punish him for his naughtiness but feels guilty that she is failing to bring him up correctly.

Author's Anecdote

St. Petersburg, the setting for *The Adventures of Tom Sawyer*, is very much like the author's home town of Hannibal, Missouri, located just north of St. Louis. In the preface to the book, Twain tells readers that some of the events in the book really happened and the characters are based on real people he knew in Hannibal. In fact, Twain writes that Tom Sawyer "is a combination of the characteristics of three boys whom I know." One of those is probably the author himself, who, as a child, often skipped school and played tricks on his mother—Twain's model for Aunt Polly.

Sidney ("Sid"). Tom's half-brother, Sid is a goody-goody tattle-tale whom Tom despises.

Becky Thatcher. The daughter of the wealthy and respected Judge Thatcher, Tom's girlfriend, Becky, is both sweet and pretty, but she can become jealous and angry at times. In the cave with Tom, she faces danger with courage and maturity.

Aldo Applesauce ❖ Johanna Hurwitz, 1979, contemporary realistic fiction. When Aldo Sossi (pronounced *saucy*) moves to the suburbs, he is nervous about joining a fourth-grade class already in progress. He is right to worry.

Aldo. Nothing goes right for Aldo with his new teacher and classmates. First, his dessert spills, and the kids tease him with the nickname "Aldo Applesauce." Then some boys play catch with his hard-boiled egg, he messes up his teacher's name, and he cannot answer when he wants to impress the teacher. As a result, Aldo is left with a lot of time to spend with his two cats and to think. He thinks about why he is a vegetarian, and whether there are animals on other planets.

DeDe Rawson. The only bright light in Aldo's life is DeDe Rawson, the girl he sits next to in class. Everyone else describes DeDe as strange, and Aldo thinks that she is indeed strange for wearing a fake mustache. He learns the truth behind the mustache and helps her

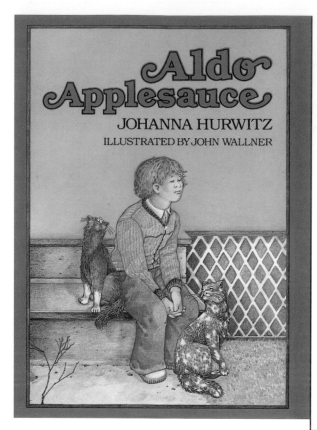

Aldo spends a lot of time with his two cats.

think about her relationship with her divorced father. She makes Aldo realize that having a nickname can be positive.

Alice's Adventures in Wonderland ❖ Lewis Carroll

(pen name for Charles Lutwidge Dodgson), 1865, fantasy/science fiction/imaginative fiction. Alice's adventures begin when she follows a talking white rabbit to his hole—and falls in. She finds herself in a magical world full of strange creatures. Alice's experiences in Wonderland include changing her size, becoming

gigantically tall or so tiny she almost disappears. More of Alice's adventures are told in *Through the Looking Glass*.

Alice. Seven-year-old Alice is so curious that she is willing to jump into a hole even if she does not know how she will get out. She is a polite child who always minds her manners, even when she finds herself in ridiculous circumstances. Alice is a spunky girl. She stands up to the Queen of Hearts, stating that the Queen is talking nonsense.

The White Rabbit. The White Rabbit, who first leads Alice into Wonderland, is a fussy, timid creature who carries a watch and worries about being late for his appointment.

From the Critics

Generations of readers have loved *Alice's Adventures in Wonderland*. One reader writes:

> I first discovered Alice from the Walt Disney animated movie, and simply had to read the book, as soon as my Mom told me that it was a book (I was in Grade Two at the time). I can't really find the right words to describe it, so all I can say is to read it for yourself and you'll never regret your journey to Wonderland.

An illustration by John Tenniel for *Alice's Adventures in Wonderland.*

The Caterpillar. The three-inch-tall Caterpillar, whom Alice meets when she is the same height, gives Alice useful information while puffing on his water-pipe.

The Cheshire Cat. The Cheshire Cat puzzles Alice because his thinking, like so much else in Wonderland, seems to make no sense. He has the annoying habit of disappearing, leaving behind only his smile.

The Queen of Hearts. The Queen of Hearts has an explosive temper and is forever demanding that anyone who offends her even slightly have his or her head chopped off.

The Mad Hatter. The Mad Hatter is the host of a tea party where all the guests, except Alice, behave like spoiled children.

All-of-a-Kind Family

❖ Sydney Taylor, 1951, historical/period fiction. In New York City in 1912–13, life is hard for a poor Jewish family like the All-of-a-Kind family. Their name comes from the fact that all five daughters dress alike.

Ella. Twelve-year-old Ella, the oldest sister, is a serious girl who is a talented actress and singer.

Henny. Henny—short for Henrietta—is ten, a mischievous girl who loves sweets and refuses to share a bed with her sisters.

Sarah. Eight-year-old Sarah's strong principles require her to pay for a lost library book herself.

Charlotte. Imaginative Charlotte, six, invents games and stories to amuse her little sister.

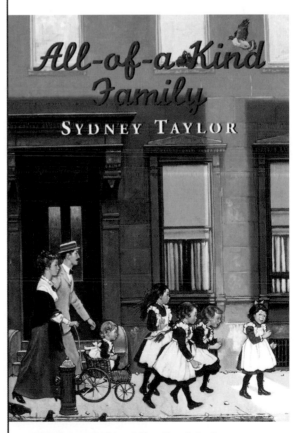

All five of the All-of-a-kind daughters show up on this cover.

Gertie. Gertie, four, is timid, finding the noise of a fire engine frightening. She worries that a new baby will replace her.

Mama. Mama enforces family rules but is also loving and compassionate.

Papa. Papa is a gentle, devout man whose honesty earns him respect among the peddlers who bring him the goods he sells.

Amber Brown Is Not a Crayon

❖ Paula Danziger, 1994, contemporary realistic fiction. Amber and her friend Justin make a great team. For example, Amber eats the filling of cookies, and Justin eats the outsides. But now, Justin is about to move away. Each friend is acting as if he or she will not miss the other one, and they wind up having an argument about something silly. Both find out that, as the cover of one edition of the book says, "Fighting with your best friend is no fun."

Amber Brown. This character is a "messy third-grader" with "brown, slightly messy hair." She has strong opinions, so when she finds out that Justin is moving, she wants to talk about it. Amber finally learns the difference between just talking and really expressing one's feelings.

Justin Daniels. Less talkative and outgoing than his friend Amber, Justin does not want to discuss the move at all. Justin, too, finds com-

PAULA DANZIGER

AMBER BROWN IS NOT A CRAYON

Amber Brown is described as having "brown, slightly messy hair."

fort when he finally realizes the importance of expressing one's true feelings.

Amelia Bedelia

❖ Peggy Parish, 1963, humorous fiction. Housekeeper **Amelia Bedelia** drives her employer, **Mrs. Rodgers**, crazy—because Amelia Bedelia obeys instructions just a little too well. If Mrs. Rodgers says, "Dress that salad," Amelia Bedelia puts clothes on it! When she is told to "ice a cake," Amelia Bedelia places it in the freezer! But Mrs. Rodgers puts up with Amelia Bedelia because she works hard and is a wonderful cook.

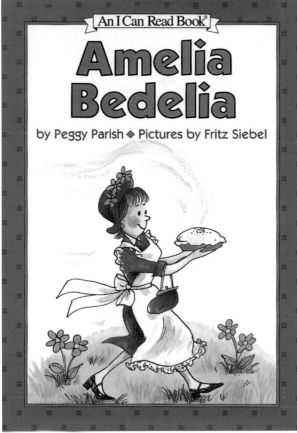

Amelia Bedelia with hat, purse, apron, and pie.

Anastasia Krupnik ❖

Lois Lowry, 1979, contemporary re-alistic fiction, ALA Notable Chil-dren's Book. To comment on events and people in her life, ten-year-old Anastasia Krupnik keeps a journal in a green notebook, listing things that she loves or hates. Her "hate" list includes the name "Anastasia" and her fourth-grade teacher, who gave her an "F" on a writing assign-ment. Anastasia also worries about the coming arrival of a new baby brother or sister and resents her parents for not consulting her about this addition to the family. She finds, however, that her attitudes change as she learns and grows.

Anastasia Krupnik. Anastasia is a bright, sensitive girl who spends much time in self-examination. She has frequent emotional shifts that are often confusing.

Although Anastasia's "hate" list is longer than the list of things she loves, she is a caring and considerate person who learns to love babies and

Anastasia experiences upsetting times as she becomes a teenager.

From the Critics

Many readers of *Anastasia Krupnik* have grown up and passed the book on to their children. One such reader writes:

> I first read this book at the age of eight. . . . This was a series I read and reread. I am now saving these books for my daughter—who, by the way, I named Anastasia. *Anastasia Krupnik* is a wonderful character who will always warm my heart. Lois Lowry created a gem.

to treat her elderly grandmother with affection and respect.

Dr. Myron Krupnik. Dr. Krupnik, Anastasia's father, is a poet and university English professor. He encourages Anastasia's poetic gift.

The Grandmother. Mr. Krupnik's mother is 92 years old. At first, Anastasia finds it hard to spend time with her because the elderly woman is often forgetful and has unpleasant habits, like talking with her mouth full. But Anastasia learns to look past these relatively unimportant matters and to sympathize with the burdens that come with age.

Mrs. Westvessel. Anastasia's fourth-grade teacher, Mrs. Westvessel, arouses mixed feelings in Anastasia. However, Anastasia learns that first impressions can be misleading when Mrs. Westvessel expresses sympathy to Anastasia on the death of Anastasia's grandmother. [*See also* THE GIVER and NUMBER THE STARS by Lois Lowry.]

Anne of Green Gables ❖

Lucy M. Montgomery, 1908, historical/period fiction. Elderly Matthew Cuthbert asks an orphanage to send a boy to help him and his sister with farm work. He is startled when it sends a girl instead. Young Anne Shirley's personality quickly wins

Anne of Green Gables takes place in Prince Edward Island.

Author's Anecdote

Lucy M. Montgomery, author of *Anne of Green Gables*, based the book on her own childhood experiences. She was raised by her grandparents on Prince Edward Island, where the story takes place. It is possible that her grandparents may have been the models for Matthew and Marilla Cuthbert. The real Green Gables Farmhouse, which is believed to be the setting for the novel, is located on Prince Edward Island and is now a museum.

Matthew over, but her ignorance of the customs of Prince Edward Island, where the farm is located, leads people to disapprove of her. Anne eventually learns from her mistakes and becomes accepted into the community.

Anne Shirley. Raised in an orphanage, Anne Shirley is by nature high-spirited.

Matthew Cuthbert. Matthew is an elderly bachelor, outwardly quiet but kind and caring.

Marilla Cuthbert. Matthew's sister is more severe than Matthew.

Are You There God? It's Me, Margaret. ❖

Judy Blume, 1970, contemporary realistic fiction. Eleven-year-old Margaret Ann Simon has a lot of worries. Her friends are developing physically into real teenagers, and she is not keeping up. They also seem to know more about boys than she does. She is also concerned about religion. Her father, who is Jewish, and her mother, who was raised Christian, believe that Margaret should choose a religion by herself.

Margaret Ann Simon. Margaret keeps her worries private, confiding in neither her parents nor her friends. Her goal is to be just like other girls.

Margaret would like to be like her friends.

Other Works by Judy Blume

Blubber
Deenie
Freckle Juice
Here's to You, Rachel Robinson
Starring Sally J. Freedman as Herself
Summer Sisters
Tales of a Fourth Grade Nothing

Nancy Wheeler. A classmate of Margaret's, Nancy, with her terrific hair and figure, seems the kind of girl that Margaret wants to be.

Laura Danker. Laura, another classmate, is tall and mature for her age.

Sylvia Simon. Margaret's paternal grandmother, Sylvia Simon, is a strong influence on her granddaughter, exposing Margaret to New York City's attractions and discussing Judaism with her.

Mr. and Mrs. Hutchins. The Hutchinses are Margaret's maternal grandparents and devout Christians who have never forgiven their daughter for marrying a Jewish man.

Arthur's Nose ❖ Marc
Brown, 1976, fantasy/science fiction/imaginative fiction. **Arthur** is an aardvark, and like all aardvarks, he

An aardvark has a very long nose.

has a very long nose. That nose is his problem. He does not like his aardvark snout, because it is different from the noses of his friends. Like most kids, Arthur worries about being different. So he visits a special nose doctor to try out pictures of different noses—a rabbit's nose, a rhino's nose, an armadillo's nose, and many more. The experience teaches Arthur that you do not have to be like everyone else. The author has also written other books about Arthur.

Bambi: A Life in the Woods

❖ Felix Salten, 1929, fantasy/science fiction/imaginative fiction. Bambi is a deer who grows up in the forest with his mother, the other deer, and the other forest animals. At first, Bambi's life is happy and carefree. Then he discovers the existence of a strange and powerful creature called "He"—a creature who can cause fear, suffering, and death. That creature, of course, is a man with a gun. Every now and then, the wise old Stag speaks words of wisdom to Bambi. He is preparing Bambi for the difficult and sad times he will face . . . and for the time when he will take the old Stag's place as Prince of the forest.

Bambi. As a fawn (baby deer), Bambi follows his mother everywhere, and his only interest is frolicking with the other fawns. When he grows older, Bambi changes. Although he is frightened the first time his mother leaves him alone, he soon learns to be independent and to get along on his own. As a handsome young stag, he falls in love with the beautiful Faline and courageously fights off other young stags to win her love. From his experiences with other animals and with "Him" (man), as well as from the teachings of the old Stag, Bambi learns wisdom.

Bambi's mother. Bambi's mother is a wise and loving parent. She protects Bambi when he is a baby, but she knows that she must prepare him to be on his own. Loving her child more than herself, she teaches him that, if "He" appears, Bambi must run for his life and not stop, even if he sees his mother fall.

Faline. Faline is the beautiful, bright, and lively young doe (female deer) whom Bambi loves.

Gobo. Faline's brother is cheerful, sweet, and kindhearted, but he is weak. Captured by "Him," Gobo lives with humans as a pet. When he returns to the forest, he wrongly thinks that he can trust humans.

The old Stag. Proud, handsome, and wise, the old Stag is a stern but loving teacher to Bambi. He first teaches Bambi that he must learn to get along without his mother. Later, he teaches Bambi an even harder lesson: "If you wanted to preserve yourself, if you understood existence, if you wanted to attain wisdom, you had to live alone." The most important lesson the old Stag teaches Bambi is that "He" is not all-powerful, as Bambi had thought. By showing Bambi the body of a dead hunter in the woods, he teaches the young stag that humans, too, can suffer and die, as can any animal in the forest. When the old Stag sees that Bambi understands this final lesson, he knows that he has completed his job as Bambi's teacher.

A Bear Called Paddington ❖ Michael Bond, 1958, fantasy/science fiction/imaginative fiction.

In London's Paddington Station, the Browns find a talking bear sitting on a suitcase. They take the lost bear home and adopt him, naming him after the railroad station where they found him.

Paddington Brown. Paddington looks like a bear but usually behaves like a human child. He has a talent for getting into trouble. As he says of himself, "Things are always happening to me. I'm that sort of bear." But Paddington is so friendly and polite that people want to help him. As a result, he always manages to come out on top.

Mr. and Mrs. Brown. Henry Brown is a big, jolly man who never gets angry. He is a good, kind father

From the Critics

Many readers will be familiar with *Bambi* from the famous and popular Walt Disney movie. The book, however, is very different from the movie.

Margery Fisher, the author of *Who's Who in Children's Literature* notes:

> . . . Walt Disney made no more drastic or mistaken change than when he showed Bambi as a cute, lisping celluloid puppet tituppring through a rainbow-hued landscape. A child who came to the book after seeing Disney's cartoon would find it hard to believe that Salten's young deer was the same character.

to his children, Judy and Jonathan—and to Paddington. Henry's wife, Mary Brown, is the first to help Paddington. She is kind and generous.

Mrs. Bird. The Browns' housekeeper, Mrs. Bird, is a motherly woman with twinkling eyes, who likes to spoil Paddington.

Mr. Gruber. Paddington's good friend, the antique dealer, is named Mr. Gruber. He is so polite that he calls Paddington "Mr. Brown."

Mr. Curry. The villain of the book is Mr. Curry, a busybody who is always criticizing and complaining.

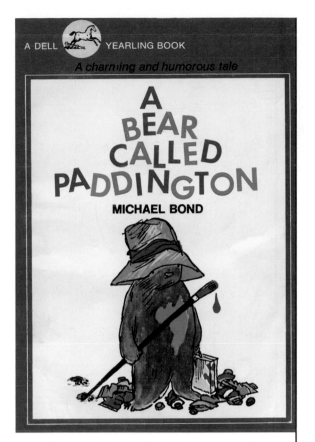

A DELL YEARLING BOOK

A charming and humorous tale

A BEAR CALLED PADDINGTON

MICHAEL BOND

Paddington Bear usually wears a hat.

Bearstone ❖ Will Hobbs, 1989, contemporary realistic fiction. Cloyd Atcitty, a 14-year-old Native American, has been in so much trouble that his tribe has sent him to a group home. There the housemother comes up with the idea to have Cloyd work for old Walter Landis, who needs help on his ranch. But Cloyd runs away into the mountains, where he finds the bearstone—a small figure of a bear carved out of turquoise. The bearstone seems like a good sign to Cloyd, and he agrees to stay on with Walter. His experiences with Walter, including brushes with death

for both of them, help Cloyd to gain confidence in himself, to trust in others, and to get his life back on track.

Cloyd. This character is a loner who doesn't trust anyone. Once Walter gains Cloyd's confidence, though, Cloyd proves himself to be loyal and hardworking. But when he feels betrayed, he gets revenge by destroying Walter's precious peach trees. Once the two reach an understanding, Cloyd shows his forgiving nature by giving the relationship another chance.

Walter. The old man treats Cloyd with love, trust, and sympathy. Even when Cloyd destroys the peach trees, Walter gets over his anger and tries to understand what was behind Cloyd's actions.

Ben and Me ❖ Robert Lawson, 1939, fantasy/science fiction/imaginative fiction. This unusual story begins with the author's statement that the book was actually written by a mouse.

Amos. The mouse, named Amos, claims that, while seeking food and shelter, he entered the home of Benjamin Franklin, the 18th-century American inventor and statesman. Amos explains how most of Ben Franklin's famous inventions and experiments—including those with electricity—were really Amos's ideas.

Ben Franklin. Amos describes Benjamin Franklin as a creative

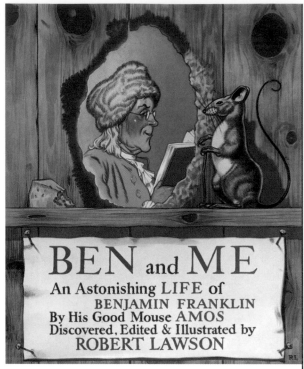

This cover shows the longer title of *Ben and Me.*

genius who lacked the sort of common sense needed to turn ideas into practical inventions. [*See also* RABBIT HILL by Robert Lawson.]

The Best Christmas Pageant Ever ❖ Barbara

Robinson, 1972, contemporary realistic fiction. The six children in the Herdman family are the town terrors. They have never even been to Sunday school, but they come this Christmas season because they hear there are refreshments and candy. When the Christmas pageant (a play about the birth of Jesus) is being planned, the Herdmans get the parts of Mary, Joseph, the Angel of the Lord, and the three wise men because the other kids are too scared to volunteer. But it turns out that the Herdmans do not even know the Christmas story. Rehearsing for the pageant, they become fascinated and ask so many questions that they get everyone else thinking about the story more than they ever had before.

Gladys. Gladys Herdman, the youngest, is also the meanest, because all the older children have taught her everything they know.

Claude. A first-grader, Claude does not know colors, shapes, ABCs, or numbers, and he has difficulty getting along with people.

The angel is a key role in *The Best Christmas Pageant Ever.*

Leroy. A third-grader, Leroy beats up on everyone and steals desserts from other kids.

Imogene. Imogene Herdman smokes cigars in the girls' room and blackmails kids.

Black Beauty ❖

Anna Sewell, 1877, fantasy/science fiction/imaginative fiction. Black Beauty, a beautiful black horse, is the central character and narrator. As he passes through the hands of a series of owners, he gets good treatment from some and abuse from others.

Black Beauty. At different times, Black Beauty is a saddle horse, a carriage horse, a cart horse, and an odd-job horse. His name changes each time he changes his owner. Throughout, he remains friendly, hard-working, and observant.

Ginger. Ginger is a horse who becomes suspicious of humans after being treated badly in early life.

Merrylegs. Merrylegs is a cheerful pony who is used to humane treatment but can protect himself from the occasional abusive rider.

John Manly. Manly is a coachman—a man who drives a coach, or horse-drawn carriage. His treatment of horses is a good example of the way all people should treat them.

Jerry Barker. Jerry drives a horse-drawn cab in the city of London. He loves his horses, talking to them and seeing that they are well fed and groomed.

Black Hearts in Battersea ❖

See THE WOLVES OF WILLOUGHBY CHASE.

The Black Stallion ❖

Walter Farley, 1941, historical/period fiction. Sailing home from India, Alec Ramsay sees a wild black stallion being loaded on board. Alec falls in love with the Black's wild beauty. When the ship sinks in a storm, Alec saves the stallion's life, and the two swim to an island, where they survive until rescued by a passing ship. Alec gets the stallion on board, and they sail to New York, where Alec tames and trains the stallion to be a champion racer.

Alec Ramsay. The book gives us three views of the red-haired, freckle-faced Alec. On the first ship, Alec shows his kindness and love for animals by befriending the Black, even though the horse is wild and violent. On the island, he proves himself to be intelligent, sensible, and resourceful by figuring out how to build a shelter and find food. He develops patience and perseverance as he gradually tames and trains the Black. And he proves his loyalty by deciding that he would starve to death rather than kill the horse for food. Back in New York, Alec's determination and single-mindedness come out as he trains the Black to race the top horses in the country.

The Black Stallion. The horse is big, beautiful, and wild. Violent by

The Boggart ❖ Susan Cooper, 1993, fantasy/science fiction/imaginative fiction, ALA Notable Children's Book. In this book, the Boggart, an invisible spirit who has lived in a Scottish castle for many centuries, is accidentally transported to the home of the Volniks, a modern family in Toronto.

The Boggart. The author describes the Boggart as "a very ancient mischievous thing, solitary and sly, born of magic as old as the rocks and the waves." He has the ability to take on various shapes and to communicate with people even though he cannot talk.

Emily Volnik. Emily is a typical 12-year-old who sometimes gets annoyed with her parents. Even though Emily is blamed for the Boggart's tricks, she becomes attached to him and comes to love his mischief.

Jessup Volnik. Ten-year-old Jessup, Emily's "pestiferous little brother," is a computer genius. He knows how to trick his parents, eats only one kind of food, and concentrates on a problem until he solves it. [*See also* THE GREY KING by Susan Cooper.]

The Book of Three ❖ Lloyd Alexander, 1964, fantasy/science fiction/imaginative fiction,

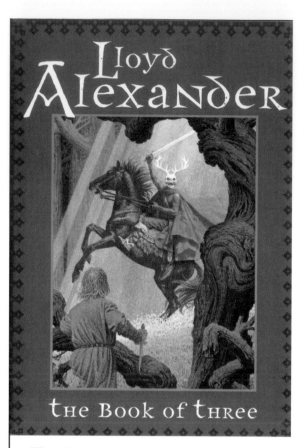

The Horned King takes center stage on this cover.

Newbery Medal. Taran, Assistant Pig Keeper to the enchanter Dallben, longs for adventure. He gets his wish when Hen Wen, a magic pig who can foretell the future, escapes from her pen. Trying to find her, Taran is attacked and wounded by the forces of the Horned King, who is the war leader for Arawn, Death-Lord of Annuvin. Taran is saved by Prince Gwydion, who helps in the search for Hen Wen. The two are later joined by a strange creature named Gurgi, who is half human and half animal. The three companions must warn the people of their land (Prydain) that Arawn is preparing for an attack. In their first adventure, they are taken to the castle of the evil Queen Achren, who throws Taran into a dungeon. He is rescued by Princess Eilonwy, who gives Taran a magic sword and joins him and his company. The companions face danger and even death to save their beloved land of Prydain from the forces of evil.

Taran. Taran is impatient and immature as the story begins. He wants to be a hero but does not understand the need for education and preparation. He also needs to become a better judge of people. Taran's adventures teach him to appreciate others for their true worth, to be loyal, and to admit his own mistakes.

Prince Gwydion. A warrior and a magician, Gwidion never gives up fighting for good and against evil. He teaches Taran that even a hero must know his own weaknesses and fear the forces of evil.

Gurgi. The furry creature Gurgi becomes Taran's faithful companion. Although Gurgi sometimes acts cowardly, he can overcome his fears and fight bravely. Most important, he has "the wisdom of a good and kindly heart."

Eilonwy. Tall and beautiful with golden-red hair, Eilonwy is independent, courageous, intelligent, and practical. Eilonwy has magical powers but does not want to become an enchantress. She prefers to fight the forces of evil along with Taran and his companions.

Arawn, Death-Lord of Annuvin. The evil Arawn is able to take many forms. His warriors—the "Cauldron-Born"—were once dead people whom Arawn has changed into cruel and powerful killers.

The Horned King. The Horned King is Arawn's war leader. His appearance alone is terrifying. He is huge and wears a bright red cloak and a mask made from the skull and antlers of a stag.

Queen Achren. Beautiful but cruel, Achren taught Arawn his magical powers but now wants revenge because he behaved ungratefully.

Fflcwddur Fflam. This character is a king who prefers to be a traveling bard. He carries a harp whose strings break every time he stretches the truth.

The Borrowers ❖ Mary Norton, 1952, fantasy/science fiction/imaginative fiction, ALA Notable Children's Book. Borrowers are tiny people, only six inches tall, who live by borrowing things from human homes. The Clocks are a family of Borrowers who live under the floorboards of an old English country house. Pod is the father; Homily, the mother; and Arrietty, their daughter.

The Borrowers live under the floorboards of an old English house.

Although girl Borrowers are not permitted to leave their homes, Arrietty finally gets permission from Pod to go borrowing with him, and she meets the boy who lives in the house. The two form a close friendship, but the Clocks are endangered when Arrietty is spotted by the mean housekeeper, who is determined to exterminate them.

Arrietty. Bored and lonely, Arrietty longs for friendship and adventure. The happiest moment of her life is when she is first allowed to leave her dark home and visit the house.

There, she begins to learn about the world. She finds out that there are more humans in the world than Borrowers and that not all humans are frightening.

The boy. The boy is a sickly child who is as lonely as Arrietty. He shows his friendship for her and her family by bringing them gifts. He shows cleverness and courage when he tries to save the Clocks from extermination by the housekeeper.

The Boxcar Children ❖

Gertrude Chandler Warner, 1950, contemporary realistic fiction. The four Alden children, on their own since the death of their parents, are worried that they will be sent to a "home" and then split up. So they set

Silhouettes of the four Alden children.

up housekeeping in an old railroad boxcar they find in the woods.

Henry. The oldest of the Alden children, Henry is responsible and mature. He looks out for the welfare of the younger children.

Jessie. This character is the older of the two girls in the Alden family. She considers it her responsibility to make sure all the children have the necessities of life—food, clothes, and a safe place to live.

Violet. Quiet and shy, Violet is also sweet, kind, and thoughtful. In addition, she is musically talented and a naturally gifted nurse.

Benny. The youngest in the family, he is lively and adventurous and makes the other children laugh.

Bridge to Terabithia

❖ Katherine Paterson, 1977, contemporary realistic fiction, Newbery Medal. Young Jess Aarons makes a friend of Leslie Burke, whose family is new in their rural Virginia community. Leslie encourages Jess's interest in art, of which his father disapproves. For his part, Jess helps Leslie deal with other kids' bullying and teasing. The two create a special place for themselves when Leslie invents an imaginary kingdom called Terabithia. To get to Terabithia and the "castle" Jess builds from scrap wood, they must swing on a rope over a dangerous gully. But Terabithia is no protection from the

real world, and Jess has to deal with tragedy and loss. In doing so, he finds unexpected inner strength and discovers that his father cares more for him than he realized.

Jess Aarons. Ten-year-old Jess feels cut off from his father and classmates. Only Leslie Burke and a teacher, Miss Edmunds, sympathize with his love for art. Though Jess secretly fears that he is a coward, he finds the nerve to defend Leslie from school bullies. He dreads swinging on the rope that he must use to reach Terabithia but manages to do it.

Leslie Burke. Leslie is an imaginative, athletic girl who becomes a target for hostility from local children when she accidentally violates

Other Works by Katherine Paterson

The Angel and the Donkey
Celia and the Sweet, Sweet Water
Come Sing, Jimmy Jo
Flip-Flop Girl
THE GREAT GILLY HOPKINS
Jacob Have I Loved
Jip: His Story
The King's Equal
LYDDIE
The Master Puppeteer
Park's Quest
Preacher's Boy
Who Am I?

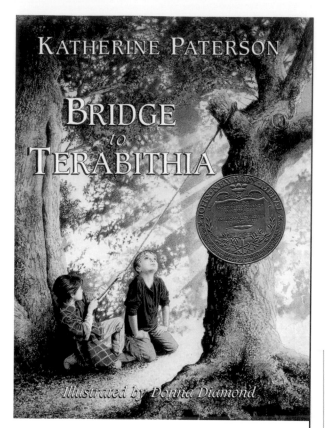

A tree and a rope are central to
Bridge to Terabithia.

unwritten rules, such as taking a bus
seat that another girl considers hers.

Mr. Aarons. Jess's father seems
harsh toward his son. The struggle
to provide for his family has left the
father angry and impatient. But
when Jess needs his love and support, Mr. Aarons shows his underly-
ing feelings for the boy.

Janice Avery. Janice is a plump,
frizzy-haired girl who can be mean
and tells lies.

Bud, Not Buddy ❖ Christo-
pher Paul Curtis, 1999, contemporary realistic fiction, ALA Best Book
for Young Adults, Coretta Scott
King Award, Newbery Medal. Bud,
the ten-year-old narrator, tells readers he was only six when his mother
died. Over the next four years, during the 1930s Depression—a period
of poverty for many people—he runs
away from the Children's Home and
several foster homes in Flint, Michigan. His goal is to find the man he
thinks is his father.

Bud. Bud is very good at describing his feelings. He tells readers, for example, "I went from kind
of calm to being in that stand-in-one-

Bud, Not Buddy takes place in the
1930s.

From the Critics

Curtis admits that two characters are based on his two grandfathers. Learning this fact, Hazel Rochman, a critic for *Booklist* magazine, wrote, "So it's not surprising that the rich blend of tall tale, slapstick, sorrow, and sweetness has the wry, teasing warmth of family folklore."

place-with-spit-drooling-down-the-front-of-your-shirt kind of scared." His imagination never stops; he figures that losing teeth when you are little means you will next lose other body parts.

Bud's outstanding trait is surviving. He copes with adults by using Rules and Things for Having a Funner Life and Making a Better Liar Out of Yourself.

Herman E. Calloway. The man Bud thinks is his father appears cold and impatient. As the book ends, Bud and the reader see a different side of Mr. Calloway. [*See also* THE WATSONS GO TO BIRMINGHAM by Christopher Paul Curtis.]

Bunnicula: A Rabbit Tale of Mystery ❖ James Howe and Deborah Howe, 1979, fantasy/science fiction/imaginative fiction, ALA Notable Children's Book. After seeing the movie *Dracula* at a

theater, the Monroe family finds a rabbit and brings it home. The rabbit, which the family names **Bunnicula,** escapes from its cage at night and sucks the juice from vegetables, leaving them white. **Harold,** the family dog and the story's narrator, is puzzled by this weird behavior. **Chester,** the family cat, is hostile to and suspicious of Bunnicula. Is Bunnicula from Transylvania, like Dracula himself? Why would a normal rabbit need a liquid diet? Despite Bunnicula's strange ways, he and Harold become friends. Chester never trusts Bunnicula and keeps trying to "rescue" the Monroes from the threat of a vampire rabbit. His plans backfire, and instead of being a hero, Chester winds up looking foolish.

Other Works by James Howe

Bunnicula Strikes Again!
The Day the Teacher Went Bananas
Eat Your Poison, Dear: A Sebastian Barth Mystery
Harold and Chester in Creepy-Crawly Birthday
Harold and Chester in The Fright before Christmas
Harold and Chester in Scared Silly
Howliday Inn
Nighty-Nightmare
Rabbit-Cadabra
There's a Monster under My Bed

Caddie Woodlawn ❖ Carol
Ryrie Brink, 1935, historical/period fiction, Newbery Medal. Caddie Woodlawn, her parents, and six brothers and sisters live in nineteenth-century Wisconsin. Life is harsh and sometimes risky, with natural disasters always a threat. Indians live in the area and are regarded by most settlers (but not Caddie) as savage and dangerous.

Caddie (Caroline Augusta) Woodlawn. Eleven-year-old Caddie is a free-spirited girl who plays with her brothers, though Mrs. Woodlawn thinks Caddie should be more ladylike. Caddie resists her mother's insistence that she give up rough play, unbecoming in young ladies. Caddie has her own mind. For example, she befriends Indian John and his family, whom neighbors fear as savage. Sensitive and caring, she buys gifts for Indian John's children and rides to warn the Indians when neighbors plot to kill them.

Johnny Woodlawn. Though descended from English nobility, Caddie's father believes in democracy. Highly respected in the community, Mr. Woodlawn has a strong influence on Caddie.

Harriet Woodlawn. Caddie's mother tries unsuccessfully to make Caddie follow traditional rules of conduct that Mrs. Woodlawn herself learned as a child in Boston.

Indian John. John becomes friendly with Caddie and urges peace and cooperation between Indians and the settlers who have moved into the area.

Call It Courage ❖ Armstrong Sperry, 1940, historical/period fiction, Newbery Medal. When Mafatu was three years old, he almost drowned, and his mother died saving him. Since then, he has feared the sea and is unable to live up to his name, which means "stout heart" in the language of his Polynesian island. Mafatu's father, the Great Chief Hikueru, is ashamed of him, and other boys his age do not want to be his friend. Even his one friend, Kana, makes fun of him because he will not go to sea with the other boys to catch fish. Mafatu runs away to another island, determined to overcome his fears and live up to his name.

Mafatu. Because the people on the island depend on the sea for food, Mafatu, who fears the sea, will never be respected as a man. His fear affects his whole life. His decision to paddle in a canoe to another island is his first act of courage. Alone on the island, Mafatu faces dangers including a wild boar, a shark, a giant octopus, cannibals—and his greatest fear, the sea itself.

The Call of the Wild ❖
Jack London, 1902, historical/period fiction. The four-year-old dog Buck, half Saint Bernard and half Scottish Shepherd, is stolen from his comfort-

able California home to work as a sled dog during the gold rush in the Far North. Buck, who eventually fights his way to the position of lead dog, is overworked and abused by a series of cruel masters. Then he meets John Thornton, the man who becomes his beloved friend, protector, and final master.

Buck. Buck shows many human characteristics. After his life of luxury, Buck discovers that life can be hard and cruel, but he accepts his situation and does what he must to survive. When he meets John Thornton, Buck proves himself a loyal and devoted friend by twice saving Thorn-

Buck, half Saint Bernard and half Scottish Shepherd, longs to return to his ancestors.

Other Works by Jack London

The Iron Heel
The People of the Abyss
The Sea Wolf
The Son of the Wolf (short stories)
White Fang

ton's life and by using every bit of his strength to help Thornton win a bet. His final act of loyalty to his master is one of revenge. With all his human qualities, Buck also feels deep within him the call of his wild ancestors to return to the wilderness.

John Thornton. The adventurous loner John Thornton rescues Buck from harsh owners. Refusing to sell Buck, even when he is offered a thousand dollars for him, Thornton returns the love and loyalty that Buck feels for his master.

The Cay ❖ Theodore Taylor, 1969, historical/period fiction. During World War II, an 11-year-old American boy, Phillip Enright, has been living on a Caribbean island with his parents. When the ship taking Phillip and his mother back to the United States is sunk by a German submarine, Phillip is knocked unconscious and blinded. He comes to on a raft with Timothy, a black man who worked on the ship. Phillip feels disdain for Timothy, even though, when they land on an uninhabited cay, or small island, Timothy protects and cares for Phillip. Then Phillip's attitudes begin to change.

Philip. Phillip is not prejudiced at first, but, influenced by his mother's attitudes, he has come to look down on black people. On the cay with Timothy, he resents being dependent on a black man who has never even learned to read. But his experiences on the cay change his way of thinking. He gains respect for Timothy's courage, intelligence, kindness, and unselfishness and cures Phillip of racial prejudice.

Charlie and the Chocolate Factory ❖ Roald Dahl,

1964, fantasy/science fiction/imaginative fiction. Charlie Bucket lives with his parents and grandparents. Since Charlie's father lost his job, life has been hard. However, Charlie's life takes a turn for the better when he finds a golden ticket in a chocolate bar. This makes him one of five lucky children who have won a contest organized by Willy Wonka, a chocolate maker. The winners receive a lifetime supply of chocolate and a tour of the chocolate factory.

Charlie Bucket. Charlie is a well-behaved and polite little boy who is good to his parents and grandparents. His self-control is so

Charlie wins a tour of the amazing chocolate factory.

strong that he makes the candy bar he receives on his birthday last a whole month.

Willy Wonka. Willy is a brilliant but peculiar inventor. His specialty is the creation of sweet treats that children love. He seems to be jolly, always laughing and smiling, but he hates to be interrupted and hates even more to be disobeyed. When a child breaks his rules, he or she can expect a terrible punishment. To the rare child who behaves perfectly, Willy is amazingly generous.

Grandpa Joe. Charlie's Grandpa Joe is ninety-six-and-a-half years old. Though he has been confined to bed for years, the chance to join Charlie on the tour of the chocolate factory leads to a miraculous recovery. He displays more common sense than the other children's companions on the tour.

Augustus Gloop. Augustus is a little glutton whose greed during the tour leads to disaster.

Veruca Salt. Veruca, a selfish, spoiled girl, throws tantrums when she cannot get her way. She wins the contest when her wealthy father buys millions of chocolate bars in order for her to find a golden ticket.

Violet Beauregarde. Violet loves to chew gum more than anything else. She will do anything to try a new flavor of gum—including disobey Willy Wonka.

Mike Teaves. Mike cares only for television, which he watches all the time, and cap pistols. [*See also* JAMES AND THE GIANT PEACH by Roald Dahl.]

From the Critics

Most of the reviews for *Charlie and the Chocolate Factory* were excellent. The *New York Times* wrote:

Candy for life and a tour of Willy Wonka's top-secret chocolate factory [were] the prize for buying a candy bar containing a Golden Ticket. Here is the exciting, hilarious, and moral story of the five prizewinners. They were, alas, repulsive children, with the exception of Charlie Bucket, whose family was so poor he could only have one candy bar a year. Rich in humor, acutely observant, Dahl lets his imagination rip in fairyland.

Charlotte's Web ❖ E. B. White, 1952, fantasy/science fiction/imaginative fiction, Newbery Honor Book.

This is the story of two friends: Charlotte, a spider with a gift for writing, and a pig named Wilbur. As the runt of his litter, Wilbur is considered useless and condemned to be killed until young Fern Arable persuades her father to spare him. Instead, Wilbur becomes the property of Fern's uncle and lives in the uncle's barn. Here, Wilbur gets to know and become friends with Charlotte. When Charlotte learns that Wilbur is due to be slaughtered for meat, she decides to try to save him and writes "SOME PIG" in a web near Wilbur, making the pig famous.

Wilbur. Like other animals in this book, Wilbur has human qualities. He is lonely until Charlotte comes into his life and becomes his friend. The spider also helps him gain self-confidence and feel better about himself, thanks to the words of praise she spins into her webs. Wilbur, who starts out thinking mostly about himself, discovers what it is to love another.

Charlotte. Charlotte is a gray spider with a large vocabulary. She has motherly feelings toward Wilbur and wants nothing more than to protect him from the fate that awaits most pigs: being slaughtered for meat. Also, she knows how to trick humans into keeping Wilbur alive. She realizes that, by spelling words out in her webs, she will make Wilbur special and important in people's eyes and persuade them that he is more

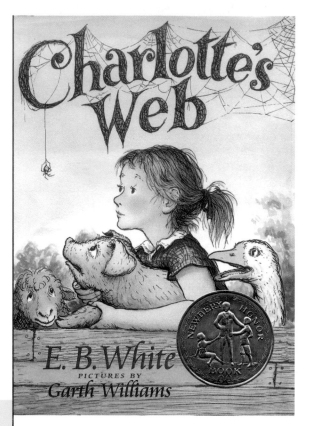

Fern and Charlotte the gray spider understand the value of life.

valuable alive than dead. Unlike Wilbur, she understands the meaning of death in Nature. As a predator, she must kill flies in order to survive.

Fern Arable. Fern is eight years old and, even though she is a farm girl, does not accept the idea that a runt pig like Wilbur usually is killed because he has little value. She understands that animals can have value beyond what they are worth for food or work.

Templeton. Templeton is a rat who demonstrates that not all animals in the world are virtuous. He is

From the Critics

When it was first published, *Charlotte's Web* received almost unanimous praise from the critics. Writing in the *New York Times Book Review*, novelist Eudora Welty said of it:

> This book has liveliness, . . . tenderness and unexpectedness, grace and humor and praise of life, and the good backbone of succinctness [shortness and clearness] that only the most highly imaginative stories seem to grow.

selfish and untrustworthy, and, when he saves Charlotte's life at one point, he does so accidentally. [*See also* STUART LITTLE by E. B. White.]

Child of the Owl ❖ Lau-
rence Yep, 1977, realistic fiction, Boston Globe–Horn Book Award. Twelve-year-old Casey Young lives with her grandmother, Paw-Paw Low, in San Francisco's Chinatown. Casey has no mother, and her father, Barney, is a hopeless gambler.

Casey. Most readers will like Casey right away. Intelligent, cre-

Chinese heritage plays an important role in *Child of the Owl.*

ative, independent, and tough, she is an honest, straightforward person who says what she thinks and hates all forms of phoniness. She loves her father, in spite of his irresponsible ways, but develops a strong dislike for her successful uncle and his family.

Paw-Paw Low. Casey's grandmother is a lot like Casey. She teaches Casey to be proud of her Chinese heritage. Her wisdom helps Casey find the strength to forgive her father for his weaknesses.

Barney. Casey's father fell into a life of gambling after serving in World War II, when he was unable to find a job because of his race. While he loves his daughter and wants to improve his life, he has a hard time changing his bad habits. [*See also* DRAGONWINGS by Laurence Yep.]

A Christmas Carol ❖
Charles Dickens, 1843, historical/ period fiction. It is Christmas Eve, but the occasion is not as happy as Bob Cratchit would like. His family lives in poverty, thanks largely to his employer, Ebenezer Scrooge. Scrooge is a nasty miser who cares nothing for Christmas and pays barely enough for the Cratchits to survive. Still, Bob Cratchit goes home determined to make the holiday as festive as possible. Scrooge expects the day to be like any other, but when Jacob Marley, his former business partner, visits, it is a

shock—because Marley is dead and is a ghost. Marley warns Scrooge to change his ways and adds that Scrooge can expect three more ghosts to visit and persuade him to reform.

Ebenezer Scrooge. Scrooge seems to care for nobody and nothing—except making as much money and spending as little as he can. But Scrooge was not always so cold and heartless. It is possible that, even now, he has feelings that he might rediscover.

Bob Cratchit. Bob Cratchit is cheerful and incapable of bitterness. He loves his family deeply and is so charitable that he does not even hate Scrooge, whose stinginess has kept his family in poverty.

Mrs. Cratchit. Bob Cratchit's wife is as sweet and cheerful as her husband and is also an expert house-maker. She is somewhat less forgiving toward Scrooge than her husband.

Tiny Tim. Tim is Bob Cratchit's youngest child, whose delicate health and physical handicap—he requires a crutch and iron braces—do not keep him from being happy.

Marley's Ghost. In life, Jacob Marley was like Scrooge in his passion for money. Now that he is dead, he realizes that his life might have had more value, to himself and others, if he had behaved differently. He wants Scrooge to have the benefit of his own knowledge.

The Ghost of Christmas Past. This spirit appears as an old man with a white beard and has the power to show events that happened in the past.

The Ghost of Christmas Present. This ghost looks like a jolly man who loves good food and companions and can show events that are currently taking place elsewhere.

The Ghost of Christmas Future. This phantom is frightening to look at, draped in long, dark robes that hide its features. It has the

This illustration captures an English Christmas of another century.

Author's Anecdote

Charles Dickens, who wrote *A Christmas Carol*, was the son of a man who had trouble making and saving money and even went to prison for his debts. At the age of twelve, young Charles had to go to work gluing labels on bottles of shoe polish. He retained a vivid memory of his early poverty, and much of his writing, like this story, focuses sympathetically on the sufferings of poor people.

power to show events that might take place at some time to come.

Chronicles of Narnia ❖
See THE LION, THE WITCH AND THE WARDROBE.

The Courage of Sarah Noble ❖ Alice Dalgliesh, 1954, historical/period fiction, Newbery Honor Book. **Sarah Noble** and her family actually lived in colonial America, although much of this book is fiction. Eight-year-old Sarah goes with her father, **John,** into the Connecticut wilderness to cook for him while he builds a house. Sarah must confront wild animals and overcome her fear of the American Indians. The Indians turn out to be friendly, and when her father goes to fetch their family, Sarah agrees to stay with an Indian she knows as Tall John. Sarah remains brave and learns about the Indians' way of life.

The Cricket in Times Square ❖ George Selden, 1960, fantasy/science fiction/imaginative fiction, Newbery Honor Book. Chester Cricket, a country cricket from Connecticut, is trapped in a picnic basket and brought back to New York City on a train. He ends up in the Times Square subway station, where he is found by Mario Bellini, a boy who works at his parents' newspaper stand. After getting permission to keep Chester at the newsstand, Mario buys him a special cricket cage to live in. In the subway station, Chester makes two friends—Tucker Mouse and Harry Cat.

Things do not go well for Chester at first. It seems that he keeps causing trouble, even though he does not mean to. It is Chester's amazing talent as a musician that saves him and brings good fortune to the Bellini family as well. In spite of the success of the wonderful concerts Chester gives in the subway station, he never stops longing for the country.

Chester Cricket. All crickets can chirp, but Chester is a musical genius who can play melodies from Italian operas! In addition to being talented, Chester is loyal and honest. He first gets into trouble by eating a

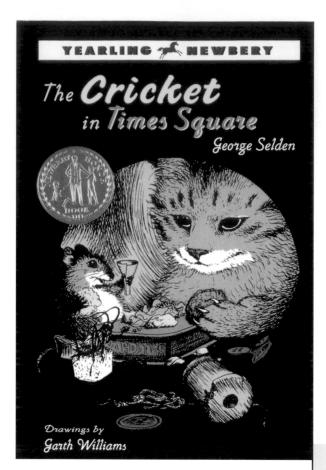

The Cricket in Times Square

George Selden

Drawings by
Garth Williams

Tucker Mouse and Harry Cat become Chester's friends.

two-dollar bill, but he refuses to blame someone else for his mistake. When he accidentally starts a fire, he uses his musical talent to earn money to save the Bellinis' newsstand. Although Chester becomes famous as a musician, he does not enjoy his success because he misses the freedom he enjoyed in the country. His love for Mario, however, makes it difficult for him to decide whether to stay at the newsstand or to take a train back to Connecticut.

Tucker Mouse. This character is a fast-talking city mouse who does not have a very well developed sense of right and wrong. When Chester eats the two-dollar bill, Tucker tries to convince him to make it look like the money was stolen by the janitor. Tucker loves Chester's music but is more interested in the money it brings in. However, he is a loyal friend who offers to help Chester escape.

Mario Bellini. Mario is a good, kind, and hard-working boy. He loves his pet cricket but does not want to keep him if it means Chester will be unhappy. Mario is able to put himself in someone else's place and imagine how a country cricket might feel living in a subway station.

From the Critics

When *The Cricket in Times Square* was first published, it was instantly popular. The *New York Herald Tribune* called it "As cheering reading as we have met in some time . . . this is absolutely grand fun for anyone. . . ." The *Saturday Review* magazine put the book in a class with one of the all-time great children's books, E. B. White's CHARLOTTE'S WEB. And the *Boston Sunday Herald* said, "There is reality here as well as delightful imagination and a story full of humor. . . ."

Dear Mr. Henshaw ❖ Beverly Cleary, 1983, contemporary realistic fiction, Newbery Medal, New York Times Notable Book. Sixth-grader Leigh Botts is unhappy in the town where he has moved with his divorced mother. He writes a letter about his problems to Boyd Henshaw, his favorite author. Mr. Henshaw advises Leigh to keep a diary.

Leigh Botts. Leigh does not think very highly of himself. He feels that other people do not notice him, and he doubts that his father loves him. He has no friends, and he worries that his parents' divorce was his fault. Then Leigh starts to feel better about himself. He begins to take pride in his own achievements and finds a friend.

Bonnie Botts. A loving mother, Bonnie Botts makes Leigh see that the divorce was not his fault.

Bill Botts. Leigh's father, Billy Botts, has never really grown up, but he does love his son.

Mr. Fridley. The custodian is a wise and caring man who teaches Leigh that his own attitude is keeping him from making friends.

Mr. Henshaw. Mr. Henshaw does not give Leigh direct advice. Rather, he helps Leigh to solve his own problems and also to develop as a writer. [*See also* HENRY HUGGINS; RAMONA QUIMBY, AGE EIGHT; and RUNAWAY RALPH by Beverly Cleary.]

Dicey's Song ❖ Cynthia Voigt, 1982, contemporary realistic fiction, Newbery Medal, Boston Globe–Horn Book Honor Book. Since Dicey Tillerman's mentally ill mother disappeared, Dicey has taken care of her younger sister and brothers. Now, with their mother dying in a mental hospital, the four children live with their grandmother.

Dicey Tillerman. Only 13, Dicey feels responsible for her family. After the children move in with their grandmother, Dicey looks forward to just being a kid. But it is hard for her to let go of responsibilities.

Gram Tillerman. Dicey's grandmother helps Dicey cope with her worries by telling her, "You've been responsible for a long time and done a good job. Take a rest now."

Dragonsong ❖ Anne McCaffrey, 1976, fantasy/science fiction/imaginative fiction, ALA Notable Children's Book, ALA Best Book for Young Adults. The setting for this novel is the planet Pern. Most people on Pern live in caves where they are safe from the deadly spores called "Thread." Thread can be destroyed only by flying, fiery dragons and the dragonriders who protect the population of Pern.

The main character is Menolly, a musically gifted teenaged girl who lives in a large cave called Half Circle Sea Hold. Menolly's harsh parents uphold the old-fashioned traditions of their male-dominated society. They forbid her to play her own music because she is a girl.

Menolly. She has the courage to run away, risking death in order to be free to play her music. Taking shelter in a cave, she nurtures nine miniature dragons ("fire lizards") and teaches them to sing. She is rescued by a dragonrider and taken to the lower caverns where society is more open-minded. The women there offer her kindness and friendship, but she still has the need to express herself through music.

Dragonwings ❖ Laurence Yep, 1975, historical/period fiction, ALA Notable Children's Book, Newbery Honor Book, Boston Globe–Horn Book Honor Book, New York Times Notable Book. Moon Shadow Lee's father, Windrider, works in a laundry in San Francisco to support his family back in China, but his dream is to build an airplane. When Moon Shadow is eight, he leaves his mother in China to live with his father.

Moon Shadow. This character is a gentle and sensitive boy, but he sticks up for his rights. He has a strong sense of fairness and honesty.

Windrider. Mr. Lee is a mechanical genius who can fix anything. He is a kind and loving father. While a dreamer, Windrider is also a hard-working, practical man.

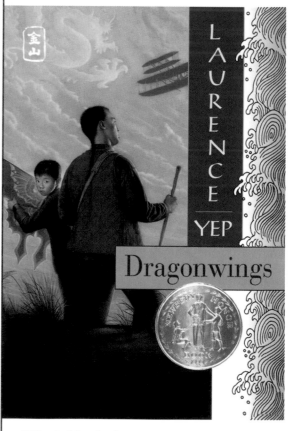

Windrider's dream is to build an airplane.

From the Critics

A reader from Atlanta, Georgia, writes:

> The story is about the life of Chinese immigrants in San Francisco early this century. It introduces a lot of Chinese culture and tradition which remind me of what I experienced in my motherland China. . . . On the other hand, it also introduces a lot of American culture from a Chinese immigrant's point of view. All in all, this is a great book.

Black Dog. The son of Windrider's Uncle Bright Star is a thug and an opium addict.

Miss Whitlaw. Kind and generous, Miss Whitlaw gives Windrider and Moon Shadow a place to live behind her boarding house. She stands up against prejudice. [*See also* CHILD OF THE OWL by Laurence Yep.]

The Egypt Game ❖ Zilpha Keatley Snyder, 1967, mystery, Newbery Honor Book. April Hall lives with her grandmother while her neglectful mother is away. April, her friend Melanie, and four other children, begin a continuing game, pretending that the yard behind the antique shop of an old man they call "the Professor" is an Egyptian temple. One night, there is a murder in the neighborhood. The players of the Egypt game solve the crime.

April Hall. Although April is starved for love, she avoids closeness with her grandmother. April hides her loneliness by wearing weird clothes and false eyelashes that are a bit crooked. Through playing the Egypt game, she learns how to get along with others.

Caroline. Caroline waits patiently for April to accept her. She never criticizes April, even when April's behavior is difficult.

Melanie Ross. Melanie, an African American girl, is a good friend who helps April to get along with other children.

The Professor. The Professor is a lonely old man who has kept to himself since his wife died. His only connection to other people comes from watching the children play.

El Bronx Remembered ❖ Nicholasa Mohr, 1975, contemporary realistic fiction, National Book Award Finalist, New York Times Notable Book. El Bronx is the name Puerto Ricans have given to the part of New York City called the Bronx. This collection of stories and a short novel takes place in the 1940s and 1950s and focuses on children or teenagers and how they act with one another and with their parents.

a novella and stories by
Nicholasa Mohr

This Puerto Rican child is one of many in the book by Nicholasa Mohr.

Little Ray. "A New Window Display" shows a group of children dealing with the topic of death as an everyday event. The story emphasizes the ability of children to bounce back and enjoy life. One key character is Little Ray, the youngest of the group and a recent arrival from Puerto Rico. Unlike most little kids, Little Ray is *not* a pest. He helps the other children with speaking Spanish. He loves the new experiences he has in New York City, always remarking, *"Qué fenomenal"* ("How phenomenal").

Encyclopedia Brown, Boy Detective ❖ Donald J. Sobol, 1963, mystery. Encyclopedia Brown opens his own detective agency and solves ten cases. The reader, too, gets a chance to be a detective and crack each case from the clues in the story.

Leroy Brown. Ten-year-old Leroy Brown is a pretty ordinary kid, but his nickname is "Encyclopedia" for a good reason. He is *really* smart. His brain clicks along like a computer, putting clues together to solve just about any mystery.

The "#1" means there are many other books about Encyclopedia Brown.

A Family Apart ❖ Joan
Lowery Nixon, 1987, historical/period fiction. In New York City, just after the Civil War, Mrs. Kelly is a young mother of six. Her husband has died, and although she works hard, she cannot support her children. Because she loves them so much, she gives them up to be adopted by families out west. The children travel by train to Missouri, where they find new homes. Frances Mary, the oldest, tells of her adventures, which include working with the Underground Railroad.

Frances Mary Kelly. Intelligent and responsible, she deeply loves her mother but cannot forgive her for breaking up the family. Frances Mary's experiences with her new family help her gain a deeper understanding of her own mother's love.

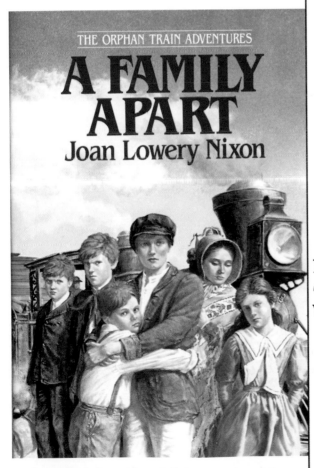

A train takes the children out west.

From the Mixed-up Files of Mrs. Basil E. Frankweiler ❖ E. L. Konigsburg, 1967, contemporary realistic fiction, Newbery Medal. Almost-12-year-old Claudia Kinkaid is bored with her life and feels unappreciated at home. She decides to teach her family a lesson in "Claudia appreciation" by running away. Because she knows her younger brother, Jamie, has money

This novel takes place in the Metropolitan Museum of Art.

saved up, she takes him with her. The two hide out in New York City's Metropolitan Museum of Art, where Claudia becomes fascinated by a small statue of an angel, carved by Michelangelo. Her curiosity about the statue and determination to find out more about it lead her and Jamie to the home of Mrs. Basil E. Frankweiler, who sold the statue to the museum.

Claudia. Claudia seems to have everything, but she does not feel special. Running away, she thinks, will make her seem more special to her family. Because she likes comfort and appreciates beauty, she chooses the museum as a hideout.

An A student, Claudia uses the museum to do research on Michelangelo. Independent and self-confident, she is not homesick or worried about being on her own.

Her experience with Mrs. Frankweiler changes Claudia in several ways. She finds the secret of the angel, not by her usual careful plan-

From the Critics

A teacher from North Carolina writes:

> I read *The Mixed-Up Files* to my fourth-grade class this past year, and we all loved it. It's one of the books that the kids beg, "Just one more chapter!" What makes it so great? First, the characters are real. The reader gets to know Claudia and Jamie as people, not just as characters in a book. Second, the idea of running away to a museum is fascinating. . . . And best of all, we loved the author's secret, which is revealed at the end of the book. Most of us were very surprised! This was a real class favorite!

ning but by following a hunch, and she realizes that her own excellent qualities are what make her special.

Jamie. Claudia's younger brother loves money, so he has saved quite a bit of it. He is the practical member of the pair, preventing Claudia from spending too much.

Mrs. Basil E. Frankweiler. A wealthy widow, Mrs. Frankweiler spends most of her time reading newspapers and filing away the articles that interest her.

Ghosts I Have Been ❖

Richard Peck, 1977, fantasy/science fiction/imaginative fiction, ALA Best of the Best, New York Times Notable Book. It is the year 1913. Most citizens of Bluff City treat Blossom Culp as an outcast. They jeer at the outlandish manners and appearance of Blossom and her mother. However, the Culps have Second Sight; they are able to see ghosts as well as look into the future and past. Blossom and her friend Alexander—who has the same gift—plunge into adventures with amazing consequences.

Blossom Culp. At 14, Blossom is tough. She refuses to give in to others' ridicule and is very quick-witted. At one point, she fakes an episode of Second Sight, claiming that her supernatural power provided information that she actually took from her teacher's desk. She rejects the passive role of "proper"

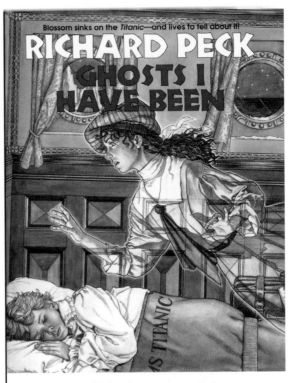

Blossom Culp has a special understanding of ghosts.

girls. In fact, Blossom scorns their genteel airs. Her strong sense of right and wrong leads her to expose a phony medium who claims to make contact with spirits of the dead.

Alexander Armsworth. This character comes from a wealthy family, but his Second Sight links him with Blossom. His feelings toward her are mixed. Because he fears ghosts, he would rather ignore his powers and resents being dragged by Blossom into scary places.

Ginger Pye ❖
Eleanor Estes, 1951, fantasy/science fiction/imaginative fiction, Newbery Medal. In this

book, the author reports not only what the main human characters think but also what goes through the mind of a dog.

Ginger Pye. The dog, Ginger Pye, sometimes comes across as quite talented. In one episode, he sets out to discover where his owner Jerry Pye disappears to each day. The dog tracks down Jerry to his classroom. In other episodes, though, Ginger does not seem too smart. For example, he thinks the dog he sees in mirrors is an enemy dog.

Jerry and Rachel Pye. Jerry, ten, and Rachel, nine, make a remarkable team. Together, they create bedtime stories about Martin Boombernickles; they decide to get a dog and earn the money to buy the puppy; and together, they search for the dog, who disappears on Thanksgiving.

Wally Bullwinkle. Another important character is Jerry's classmate Wally. The author makes readers suspect Wally by writing: "He pretended to be lost in his big geography book, but he had a hand over his face and from between his fingers he was studying Ginger with a sly and furtive mien." [*See also* THE HUNDRED DRESSES by Eleanor Estes.]

The Giver ❖ Lois Lowry, 1993, fantasy/science fiction/imaginative fiction, Newbery Medal, Boston Globe–Horn Book Award. The setting for this book is a world in which there is no pain or sickness, no war, no poverty, and no crime. Even the weather is perfect. But while life is safe and comfortable, it is also dull. People have no emotions or imaginations. Families are allowed two children, one boy and one girl, who are assigned to them. When children reach the age of 12, the Elders decide which jobs will be best for them.

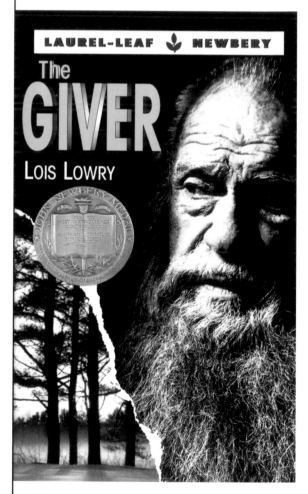

When the Receiver ages, he becomes the Giver and passes all his memories onto a young boy named Jonas.

Some become Nurturers, responsible for seeing that every child born will either be acceptable for assignment to a family or be "released," meaning killed by lethal injection.

One member of the community is called the Receiver who is the only person who remembers the past and, therefore, the only one who knows about things as happiness, sadness, pain, color, and snow. As the book opens, a boy named Jonas is almost 12, awaiting his life assignment. He is honored with the job of Receiver. The current Receiver, now old, will become the Giver, passing all his memories on to Jonas.

Jonas. Jonas is given the job of Receiver because of his intelligence, wisdom, and sensitivity. As Jonas receives the Giver's memories, he also begins to feel. And the more he feels, the less he can accept the unfeeling world in which he lives.

Asher. Jonas's best friend, Asher, is very different from Jonas. Rarely serious, he is given the job of Assistant Director of Recreation.

Fiona. Jonas's friend, Fiona, is quiet and kind. Because of her caring, sensitive nature, she is given the job of Caretaker of the Old.

Lily. Jonas's sister, Lily, is only seven years old, but she is already worried about the Ceremony of Twelve. [*See also* ANASTASIA KRUPNIK and NUMBER THE STARS by Lois Lowry.]

The Great Brain ❖ John D. Fitzgerald, 1967, historical/period fiction. This story is based on the author's childhood in Utah. The author lets seven-year-old J.D. tell the story. It is 1896, and J.D. lives in awe of his brilliant but sly ten-year-old brother, Tom. J.D. admits he cannot keep up with Tom, the Great Brain.

Tom. Somehow this character manages to solve any problem so that he comes out financially ahead and always looks like a hero. He figures out how to make money or look heroic whether he is rescuing

Tom, the Great Brain, and J.D.

friends in a cave, selling junk to a new immigrant, or masterminding a way to get rid of a teacher.

Probably, the best word to describe Tom is *conniving*, which means "secretly doing something wrong." In the last chapter, the Great Brain does reform, or improve, his behavior.

J.D. J.D. is more childish but also more honest than Tom. Sometimes J.D. is truly good, as when he refuses to take advantage of the Greek boy, who is new to town. Sometimes J.D. gets into situations that he does not fully understand. For example, when he cooperates with a friend who tries to kill himself, J.D. does not fully understand his actions. Mostly though, J.D. has a conscience.

The Great Gilly Hopkins ❖ Katherine Paterson, 1978,
contemporary realistic fiction, Newbery Honor Book, National Book Award for Young People's Literature. Gilly Hopkins has lived in foster homes since she was three, when her mother abandoned her. Her new foster mother, Mamie M. Trotter, has her hands full with Gilly.

Gilly Hopkins. Gilly is mean, hateful, and dishonest. Feeling rejected and unloved has made Gilly angry, insecure, and unpleasant. She dislikes Trotter for being fat and sloppy, and she fails to see Trotter's

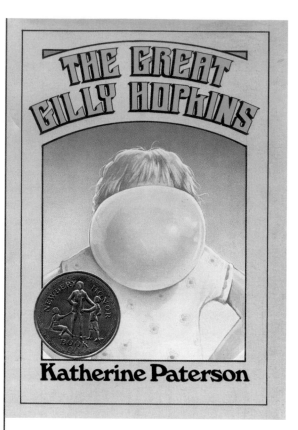

The cover illustrator decided to hide Gilly Hopkins from the reader.

more important qualities. She looks down on Trotter's other foster child, William Ernest ("W.E."), for being slow. And she hates both a neighbor, Mr. Randolph, and her teacher, Miss Harris, because they are black. Gilly daydreams about a reunion with her mother, Courtney, who she imagines is beautiful and glamorous. In a letter to Courtney, Gilly lies about being mistreated in her foster home. Courtney, who does not love or want Gilly, has "Nonnie," Gilly's grandmother, visit the Trotter home. Nonnie decides that she should take care of Gilly. The trouble is that Gilly has come to love Trotter and wants to stay with her. [*See also* BRIDGE TO TERABITHIA and LYDDIE by Katherine Paterson.]

The Grey King ❖ Susan
Cooper, 1975, fantasy/science fiction/imaginative fiction, Newbery Medal. This book is part of a series about a battle between good and evil that has raged since the beginning of time. Young Will Stanton, who fights for the forces of good, goes to Wales to recover from an illness. Guided by Professor Merriman Lyon, a wise veteran of the war between Light and Dark, Will joins another boy, Bran Davies. They search for a magic harp that can awaken the Six Sleepers, ancient figures who will aid the powers of Light. Their most dangerous opponent is the Grey King, an evil lord of the Dark.

Will Stanton. As "the seventh son of a seventh son," Will has magical powers—once he knows his real nature. On his eleventh birthday, he discovers his true identity as one of the immortal Old Ones, who serve the Light. As an Old One, Will can travel through time and communicate thoughts by telepathy.

Bran Davies. Bran is an albino, a person with white hair and skin, whose sensitive eyes require dark glasses during the day. Being albino leaves him feeling like an outsider, a sense that is reinforced when he learns who he actually is—the son of King Arthur and Queen Guinevere.

Professor Merriman ("Merry") Lyon. The Professor is actually the most powerful of the Old Ones. The clue to his real name lies in his nickname: Merry Lyon, or Merlin, the wizard who taught and then served King Arthur. The Professor's dedication to the Light means that he is sometimes not considerate of the feelings or welfare of individual persons, if harming them may serve to advance the cause of good. [*See also* THE BOGGART by Susan Cooper.]

Harriet the Spy ❖ Louise
Fitzhugh, 1964, contemporary realistic fiction, ALA Notable Children's Book. Harriet is 11 and wants to be a

Harriet, a curious 11-year-old, spies on all her classmates.

*Other Works by
Louise Fitzhugh*

The Long Secret (a sequel to *Harriet
the Spy*.)
*Nobody's Family Is Going to Change
Sport*

writer. She carries a notebook to record her thoughts and observations while spying on people.

Harriet M. Welsch. Harriet does not see spying as an invasion of others' privacy because she believes that writers should know all about people and do not have to obey rules of courtesy. Though Harriet is curious about people, she does not care much for them.

She spies on all her classmates. When other children find and read Harriet's notebook, Harriet discovers that spies are unpopular. The children start treating Harriet as an enemy, and she resents their view of her at first. Slowly, Harriet comes to appreciate that people—including Harriet herself—have feelings that must be respected.

Harry Potter and the Sorcerer's Stone ❖ J. K. Rowling, 1997, fantasy/science fiction/imaginative fiction. After Harry

Potter's parents die in a car crash when Harry is a baby, he has to live with the Dursleys, his uncle and aunt, and their son, Dudley. For ten years, the adult Dursleys treat him as an unwelcome nuisance, and Dudley makes Harry his punching bag. Everything changes when a huge, hairy man named Hagrid tells the boy that he, Harry, is . . . a *wizard*, as his parents had been. Moreover, Harry has been accepted into the Hogwarts School of Witchcraft and Wizardry.

Suddenly, Harry finds himself in the astonishing world of magic, one that exists side-by-side with the world of unknowing, nonmagical people, or "muggles," as wizards call them. In this world, wizards and witches fly on broomsticks, use owls to send messages, and cast spells with magic wands.

Harry Potter. With his glasses and messy hair, Harry looks ordinary, except for a lightning-bolt-shaped scar on his forehead.

At Hogwarts, Harry's behavior is still that of a schoolboy rather than a wizard. He is sociable and makes good friends among the students—as well as a few enemies. His natural athletic talent is such that he becomes a star at Quidditch, a sport. When danger threatens, Harry shows himself to be a boy with the courage and quick wits to meet the threats that come at him from his most dangerous enemies—especially supervillainous Lord Voldemort.

From the Critics

Almost as soon as it reached the bookstores, *Harry Potter and the Sorcerer's Stone* became hugely popular—and not only with young readers. Adults, too, have found this book delightful. One such reader wrote:

> From the moment I began reading this book I was captivated. Needless to say, Rowling's capability to hold the attention of both adult and child is truly amazing.

A child reader wrote that the book "kept me on the edge of my seat throughout the whole thing. This book took me places I have never imagined."

The Dursleys. Mr. and Mrs. Dursley and their son, Dudley, are stupid, nasty people who mistreat Harry badly. The older Dursleys have always known that Harry is a wizard but hid the fact from him because they hate anything out of the ordinary. They adore their greedy, cowardly son and spoil him shamefully.

Albus Dumbledore. This character, the Headmaster of Hogwarts, appears to be an inoffensive, elderly man. However, Dumbledore was a powerful enough wizard in his day to defeat the dreaded Lord Voldemort—for a time.

Hagrid. Hagrid, the Hogwarts Gamekeeper, is half-human and half-giant. Despite his fierce appearance, he is soft-hearted and loves all animals, even dragons.

Hermione Granger. Hermione is a bright and studious classmate of Harry's. She becomes one of his closest friends and allies at the school.

Ron Weasley. Ron, one of several Weasley children at Hogwarts, is Harry's best friend.

Lord Voldemort. This character is a wizard who turned evil. He is responsible for the death of Harry's parents. Most wizards fear Voldemort so greatly that they will not say his name aloud.

Hatchet

❖ Gary Paulsen, 1987, contemporary realistic fiction, ALA Best Book for Young Adults, Newbery Medal. When he boards the small airplane that will take him to visit his father in a remote Canadian oil field, Brian Robeson feels angry and hurt. His parents have recently divorced, and Brian's wishes were not taken into account by his parents or the judge who decreed that he must live with his mother and make periodic visits to his father. Even worse, Brian knows that his mother is in love with a strange man—which is why she had wanted the divorce.

The little plane's pilot collapses and dies while flying over the bleak wilderness, and suddenly Brian must confront far more serious issues than the divorce. He must try to land the airplane, having never even been in one before. Surviving that challenge, he must survive alone in the middle of nowhere, with neither survival gear nor wilderness experience to help him. Brian's only useful implement is the hatchet his mother had given him just before he left for Canada.

Brian Robeson. Brian must face very tough challenges: finding food and protecting himself from cold, wind, rain, and hostile animals. He learns that he has enough courage not to give in to panic and despair when he realizes that he is completely alone. He is resourceful, quick to learn, and discovers that he is a survivor.

Heidi ❖ Johanna Spyri, 1880, historical/period fiction. Heidi is a Swiss orphan living in the Alps with her Aunt Dete. When Heidi is five, she goes to live with her grandfather. Aunt Dete later takes Heidi to the city as a companion for a sickly girl named Clara. Though Heidi and Clara are friendly, Heidi misses the mountains and becomes ill. Only the healthy mountain climate and the simple country life make her truly happy.

Heidi. Lovable Heidi charms almost everyone, even her cross old grandfather. Caring deeply for nature and the simplicity of country life, Heidi feels trapped and depressed in the city. Even when un-

happy, however, Heidi always thinks first of the happiness of others.

Clara Sessemann. A little older than Heidi, Clara is an invalid—until she discovers the healing power of country air and a simple life.

The grandfather. Before Heidi comes to live with her grandfather, he avoids everyone in his mountain village, and they avoid him in return. Life has made him bitter and unhappy, but then he experiences Heidi's love and cheerful spirit.

Peter the Goatherd. Peter lives near Heidi in the Alps. Although he never really means harm to anyone, his selfishness and lazi-

Heidi and her grandfather have a special relationship.

ness contrast sharply with Heidi's sunny, considerate personality.

Henry and Mudge

❖ Cynthia Rylant, 1987, contemporary realistic fiction, ALA Notable Children's Book. **Henry** is an unhappy little boy because he has no brothers or sisters, nor are there other children to play with on his street. When his parents agree to get him a dog, he chooses a cute little puppy and names him **Mudge**. Though Mudge is tiny at first, he becomes huge. But even when he is gigantic, Mudge remains gentle and friendly. Henry, who had been timid before Mudge's arrival, becomes more sure of himself. His attachment to Mudge teaches him the importance of love and loyalty. The boy and dog become inseparable companions, walking to school together and sharing a bed, even having the same dreams. [*See also* MISSING MAY by Cynthia Rylant.]

Henry Huggins

❖ Beverly Cleary, 1950, contemporary realistic fiction. Henry Huggins finds a stray dog and gets permission from his parents to keep him on one condition. The condition is that Henry get the dog home on the bus, where dogs are not allowed. Henry wraps up the dog, pretending that he is a parcel. But the dog gets loose on the bus, and Henry finds himself in trouble.

Strange things have a way of happening to Henry, and this book describes several of them.

Henry Huggins. A third-grader, Henry never intends to cause trouble and is never mean. But nothing works out as he plans. He likes people and loves animals, even the guppies he tries to raise, with disastrous results.

Ribsy. Ribsy is Henry's devoted, loving dog, of mix breeds. Henry picks the name because the dog is so skinny. Henry thinks Ribsy is the best dog in the world.

Mrs. Huggins. Henry's mother has to be very patient with her son,

Henry Huggins tries to get his dog home on a bus.

and is. Aside from correcting Henry's mistakes in grammar, she accepts almost everything he does.

Mr. Huggins. Henry's father never loses his temper, no matter what trouble Henry gets into. He is always there with a helping hand. [*See also* DEAR MR. HENSHAW; RAMONA QUIMBY, AGE EIGHT; and RUNAWAY RALPH by Beverly Cleary.]

Hitty: Her First Hundred Years

❖ Rachel Field, 1929, fantasy/science fiction/imaginative fiction, Newbery Medal. **Hitty** is a doll who has led an eventful existence. While sitting in a New York antique shop, she tells about her life. Originally made for a seven-year-old girl in Maine, Hitty has gone to sea in a whaling ship and been rescued from a tribe in the South Seas. She becomes the property of a snake charmer in India and later poses for paintings by a famous artist. A great writer holds her in his hands, and several children own her over her hundred-year history. Through Hitty's eyes, readers are treated to a fascinating parade of history.

The Hobbit

❖ J. R. R. Tolkien, 1937, fantasy/science fiction/imaginative fiction. Bilbo Baggins is a *hobbit*—a short, plump, quiet character who does not look or behave like a hero. But he is given a task to perform that is worthy of a hero: to recover a treasure that a fierce dragon had stolen.

Bilbo Baggins. Bilbo is a typical hobbit, meaning that he dislikes danger and prefers to lead a peaceful life. However, his mother's family are the Tooks, hobbits who love adventure. As a result, this hobbit feels duty-bound to take on the dangerous job of recovering a treasure from a dragon. Though he sometimes avoids disaster by luck alone, he learns to act with courage and to master the fear that he often feels. He discovers that the bravest character is the one who acts even when he is afraid.

Gandalf. With his long, white beard, his pointed hat, and his staff, Gandalf looks like a true wizard. Not only can he use powerful magic, he can also sense qualities that nobody else is aware of. That is why Gandalf chooses Bilbo Baggins to carry out a risky task. Gandalf's advice and assistance are vital in the hobbit's early struggles, and Gandalf also helps the hobbit learn to use his own talents and skills.

Thorin Oakenshield. Thorin comes from a royal family—and makes sure that everyone knows this fact and treats him as a lord. When he actually gets power, he lets it go to his head. But in a crisis, Thorin demonstrates that he is brave and honorable.

Gollum. Gollum's odd name comes from the ugly gulping sound he often makes while talking. He is a nasty, cowardly little sneak who lives by himself underground. He has no friends and is one of Bilbo Baggins's most scheming enemies.

Holes ❖ Louis Sachar, 1998, mystery, Newbery Medal, Boston Globe–Horn Book Award, National Book Award for Young People's Literature, New York Times Notable Book. The main character—an innocent, hopeful, and overweight boy named Stanley—accepts his fate

Author's Anecdote

On the Web site of the Children's Book Council, Louis Sachar explains his writing process:

I never talk about a book until I'm finished writing it. . . . It took me a year and a half to write *Holes*, and nobody knew anything about it, not even my wife or my daughter. . . . The more you talk about something, the less you tend to do it. By not permitting myself to talk about *Holes*, I was forced to write it. The story was growing inside me for a year and a half, and I had no other way to let it out.

when he is sent to Camp Green Lake, a juvenile detention center.

Stanley Yelnats IV. In a letter home, Stanley does not tell his parents just how terrible Green Lake is, even though it has not taken him long to become suspicious of why all the "campers" must dig large holes. Then, as he sheds pounds and develops muscles, Stanley seems at first to harden his heart. He keeps to himself and turns down a plea from Zero, another boy, to teach him to read. But he later agrees to teach Zero, and when Zero runs away, Stanley cannot ignore his conscience, which tells him to track down the boy. Stanley and Zero help each other survive in the desert and come up with a plan to get back to civilization.

Holes is deeper than just a story about Stanley, the bad boys, and their guards. The author creates a historical puzzle involving characters who lived generations ago. They were not only connected to one another in the past but to this day are also connected to Stanley.

In the final section, called "Filling in the Holes," the author brings up the topic of "the change in Stanley's character and self-confidence" as a result of the Camp Green Lake experience.

The other boys at Camp Green Lake. The other boys, all of whom have nicknames, make a bully back at Stanley's school seem cute.

They speak in dialogue that rings true.

Mr. Pendanski, Mr. Sir, and the warden. The adults at the camp make life miserable for the boys. The counselor, Mr. Pendanski, tries too hard to be positive and supportive. Mr. Sir sports a tattoo of a rattlesnake and enjoys denying Stanley water. The warden polishes her nails with rattlesnake venom while waiting for the boys to dig up the treasure she has spent her life searching for. [*See also* MARVIN REDPOST: KIDNAPPED AT BIRTH? and WAYSIDE SCHOOL IS FALLING DOWN by Louis Sachar.]

Homecoming ❖ *See* DICEY'S SONG.

Homer Price ❖ Robert McCloskey, 1943, humorous fiction. Homer is a boy from a midwestern town, where he lives with his family—and his pet skunk, Aroma. The stories in this book deal with the lives of Homer and his friends and neighbors. These are not especially comical or strange people, but their habits and peculiarities create amusing and complicated situations.

Homer Price. Homer is a bright boy who builds radios from kits and is always willing to help others, although the results he gets may not be what he intended. He is more observant than some adults, recognizing qualities in others that grownups fail to notice.

The people in *Homer Price* create amusing situations.

Uncle Ulysses. Uncle Ulysses likes to invent machines that are meant to help avoid work but usually lead to disasters.

Uncle Telemachus. Uncle Telemachus collects string as a hobby and wants to marry Miss Terwilliger. He competes with the sheriff.

The sheriff. He collects string, mangles the English language, and is slow to enforce the law when doing so would interfere with his routine.

Miss Terwilliger. This character loves to knit, makes delicious fried chicken, and is the town's champion string collector.

The House at Pooh Corner ❖ *See* WINNIE-THE-POOH.

The House of Dies Drear ❖ Virginia Hamilton, 1968, mystery, ALA Notable Children's Book. The fictional character Dies Drear, who worked to abolish slavery, was murdered decades before the action of the plot begins. His deeds created the mystery that the Small family encounter when they move to Ohio and lease Drear's house, which now belongs to a foundation and may be haunted. The house itself plays a major role in this book—scaring the innocent and withholding secrets.

Thomas Small. This main character is a realistically drawn 13-year old—curious about his surroundings and worried about making friends and about his looks.

Pluto. Another main character, Pluto, lives in a cave near the house. Dressed strangely, Pluto is an elderly, ailing man. Thomas and his father, a history professor, need to figure out if Pluto is a devil or the key to the legend surrounding the house, which was a stop of the Underground Railroad. Eventually they learn that Pluto is a descendant of runaway slaves.

The Darrows. The Darrows are other neighbors, who seem mean. There is bad blood between them and Pluto. The Darrows' behavior involves pointless digging on their land, as if they are looking for something. [*See also* M. C. HIGGINS THE GREAT and ZEELY by Virginia Hamilton.]

How to Eat Fried Worms ❖ Thomas Rockwell, 1973, contemporary realistic fiction. One night Billy Forrester is punished for not eating salmon. But the next day, Billy makes a bet with Alan that he, Billy, can eat 15 worms in 15 days.

Billy Forrester. The author describes Billy as "chubby, snub-nosed, freckled." But what Billy looks like is not as important as what people say about him and how he acts. Alan is right to describe Billy as "awful stubborn." Indeed, Billy keeps to his diet of worms, sometimes boiled, sometimes fried.

Alan. The other boy in the bet is Alan, who has a different fear. He is afraid he will have to pay up the $50. So Alan and his friend Joe try to trick Billy into losing the bet. For example, they fake a letter from a doctor and stuff Billy with tons of junk food.

The Hundred and One Dalmatians ❖ Dodie Smith, 1957, fantasy/science fiction/imaginative fiction. In this novel, dogs communicate with one another and understand human speech. The Dalmatians Pongo and Missis Pongo have 15 pups. After the pups are

A dalmatian often brings to mind the classic book by Dodie Smith.

stolen, their parents must come to their rescue.

Cruella de Vil. The puppy thief is peppery Cruella de Vil, whose name (Cruel Devil) matches her personality. She values animals only for their skins, which she thinks make glamorous coats.

Pongo. With "one of the keenest brains in Dogdom," help from Missis Pongo, and a superb communication system with the other dogs, Pongo saves not only his own 15 but also dozens of other Dalmatians.

The Hundred Dresses ❖
Eleanor Estes, 1944, contemporary realistic fiction, Newbery Honor Book. This is a story about not judging people by appearances.

Wanda Petronski. Wanda is a shy, quiet girl from a poor home. She wears the same old blue dress to school every day. Nevertheless, she claims that she has a hundred beautiful dresses in her closet. Some of her classmates tease Wanda for her ridiculous claim—but Wanda will not admit that she is lying. Other students make fun of Wanda because they think the name Petronski is "funny." Although her classmates do not know it, Wanda is gifted.

Maddie. Like her friends, Maddie teases Wanda about the dresses but does not believe that she is acting cruelly. But Maddie cares too much about her friends' opinion of her to change her behavior toward Wanda, even when she doubts that it is proper. Eventually, after Maddie learns more about Wanda, she feels bad about having teased her. [*See also* GINGER PYE by Eleanor Estes.]

Characters learn and grow in *The Hundred Dresses.*

I, Juan de Pareja ❖

Elizabeth Borton de Treviño, 1965, historical/period fiction, Newbery Medal. The two main characters of this book are real people who lived in the 1600s. One is the great Spanish painter Diego Velásquez. The other is Juan de Pareja, a black man, who was a slave in the painter's household.

Juan de Pareja. Pareja narrates the story years after Velásquez's death. Pareja describes being trained to work in the painter's studio. Over time, Pareja becomes an indispensable assistant to Velásquez—and, eventually, a close friend.

Pareja is extremely intelligent and discovers that he is himself a talented painter. But he must hide his talent because Spanish law forbids slaves to learn or practice any art. This situation is only one of the terrible injustices of slavery that Pareja must face. But Juan de Pareja's intelligence, strength of character, and talents shine through, despite the cruel social system.

In the Year of the Boar and Jackie Robinson ❖

Bette Bao Lord, 1984, contemporary realistic fiction, ALA Notable Children's Book. In 1947, a Chinese girl

Shirley adjusts to her new American life.

and her mother leave China to join the girl's father in New York City. This book is the story of the girl's life in the United States.

Shirley Temple Wong. Before she leaves China, the girl's family gives her a new, "American" name: Shirley Temple Wong.

Shirley is intelligent and observant, and these qualities help her to adapt to her new home. She learns English, gets acquainted with her fifth-grade classmates, and even becomes a baseball fan.

Her new life becomes more complete when Shirley finds her first close friend, studious Emily Levy. Nevertheless, Shirley constantly looks for ways to find a balance between her cultural roots and the new life for which her American name is a symbol.

Island of the Blue Dolphins ❖ Scott O'Dell, 1961,

historical/period fiction, Newbery Medal. In the early 1800s, a woman named Karana is believed to have survived alone for 18 years on an island in the Pacific Ocean. O'Dell's idea for this novel came from the real Karana's story. In the book, 12-year-old Karana lives on an island with her father, the village chief. After the village is attacked and Karana's father killed, the new chief takes his people away. But as their boat is leaving, Karana jumps ship to join her younger brother, Ramo, who has

From the Critics

In 1976, the Children's Literature Association named *Island of the Blue Dolphins* one of the ten best American children's books in the past 200 years. A quarter of a century later, the book continues to be extremely popular among young readers.

been accidentally left behind. The ship never returns. After Ramo is killed by wild dogs, Karana survives alone for 20 years.

Karana. Karana shows courage and devotion by swimming back to the island when she sees that her brother Ramo has been forgotten. She also shows courage by fighting off the wild dogs that threaten her. Self-reliant and resourceful, Karana makes a bow and arrows and builds a home. When she rescues a wounded dog, she realizes how lonely she has been. But if she is rescued, how will she communicate with other humans after living alone for so long?

James and the Giant Peach ❖ Roald Dahl, 1961, fantasy/

science fiction/imaginative fiction. From the day when he is orphaned at the age of four (a rhinoceros eats his parents), James Henry Trotter has a miserable time living with his cruel aunts. When he is seven, James's life changes after an old man in a green suit gives him a bag of magical green objects. James accidentally spills them, and they dig themselves into the ground near a tree, which then grows an enormous peach. The boy finds a hole in the peach, crawls inside, and meets seven gigantic but friendly insects. One, a Centipede, bites through the stem of the peach. The peach rolls down a hill, killing the nasty aunts as it goes. Freed from his wicked guardians, James becomes the leader of the insects and goes on a series of weird adventures.

James Henry Trotter. Poor James gets only abuse from his guardian aunts and has no friends or fun in his life. However, from the time he crawls into the giant peach, he finds personal strengths he had never dreamed of. He is a natural leader and discovers that he is brave.

The Centipede. The Centipede wears boots on his many feet but cannot untie the laces without help. He loves fun and mischief, but his lack of self-control can cause problems. For example, he makes the Cloud-Men angry by teasing them.

The Earthworm. The Earthworm sees the gloomy side of everything. He and the Centipede quarrel constantly because the Centipede makes fun of him. Despite his pessimism, the Earthworm is brave, allowing himself to be used as bait to lure some birds.

The Ladybug. The Ladybug is gentle and kind to James when James needs reassurance and mothering. She is also vain, never letting anyone forget that ladybugs with nine spots, like her, are superior.

The Old-Green-Grasshopper. The Old-Green-Grasshopper teaches James many fascinating facts about insects. A skilled musician, he plays music by using his leg and wing as a bow and violin.

The Aunts. Aunt Sponge is short, fat, and cruel to her nephew. Aunt Spiker is tall, skinny, screechy, and cruel to her nephew. [*See also* CHARLIE AND THE CHOCOLATE FACTORY by Roald Dahl.]

Jar of Dreams ❖ Yoshiko Uchida, 1981, contemporary realistic fiction. This book is about a Japanese American girl, her family, and her community in California in 1935.

Rinko. This character is 11 and tells the story. She wants to be like everyone else, but people treat her as if she were different because she

Rinko learns to appreciate her Japanese robe like the one pictured here.

has Japanese parents. Sometimes people are cruel to her. For example, the owner of a laundry calls Rinko and her brothers and sisters "you damn Japanese kids." Rinko's dream is to be a teacher, but she worries that her dream may not come true. She also worries that her visiting aunt from Japan will be boring. At the end, she appreciates her aunt, holds on to her dreams, and puts on a kimono, a Japanese robe.

Papa. Papa is having a hard time earning a living as a barber. His dream is to open a garage and repair shop, and he claims he loves America even if he is not loved back.

Author's Anecdote

Yoshiko Uchida was born in California to parents who had come from Japan. During World War II in the 1940s, she, her family, and other Japanese Americans were sent away from their homes to internment camps because the U.S. government thought they would become spies and help the Japanese, who were the enemy during this war. Later, Uchida was able to leave the camp and go to Smith College. She became famous not only for her original stories but also for the old Japanese folktales that she collected and published for American readers.

Aunt Waka. The aunt, visiting from Japan, has lost her son and her husband. She also has a bad foot, and her hair is gray, even though she is younger than Rinko's mother. But Aunt Waka can laugh, and Rinko says she is "an OK person after all." In fact, Aunt Waka helps everyone stand up for his or her dreams.

Julie of the Wolves ❖

Jean Craighead George, 1972, contemporary realistic fiction, Newbery Medal. The main character in this book has two different names, one from each culture in her background. She was born and raised an Eskimo named Miyax. At times in her life, she lives among whites and has the name Julie Edwards.

Julie Edwards. At the age of 13, Julie runs away from an unwanted Eskimo marriage and finds herself alone without food in the harsh Alaskan wilderness. She is forced to struggle for survival with no companions except a wolf pack.

Julie finds challenges and rewards in all the communities where she lives: among Eskimos as Miyax, among Americans as Julie, and among the wolves, where she has no name at all. She recognizes the importance of names and gives names to the wolves in her adopted pack.

Of all the people who influence Julie, the most important is her Eskimo father, Kapugen, a great hunter.

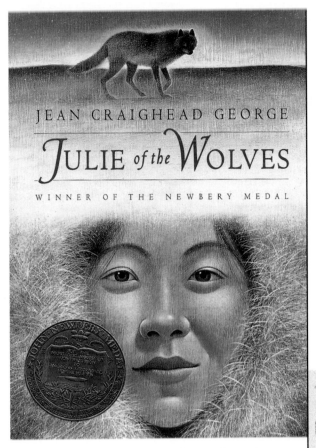

JEAN CRAIGHEAD GEORGE

JULIE of the WOLVES

WINNER OF THE NEWBERY MEDAL

Julie gives names to the wolves in her adopted pack.

[*See also* MY SIDE OF THE MOUNTAIN by Jean Craighead George.]

The Jungle Book ❖ Rud-

yard Kipling, 1894, fantasy/science fiction/imaginative fiction. When Shere Khan, a man-eating tiger, kills the parents of a young English boy in India, the boy stumbles into the lair of a pack of wolves. Mother Wolf refuses to give the little boy up to the tiger, so the wolves adopt and raise the child, naming him Mowgli, meaning "Frog." Mowgli grows up with the wolves and learns the Law of the Jungle. With a few exceptions, such as Tabaqui the jackal, the animals follow this law. Shere Khan remains Mowgli's enemy, but the boy develops many friends and allies.

Mowgli. Mowgli is too young to remember his life among human beings. From the time the wolves take him in, he thinks of himself as a wolf cub. He eats and behaves as much as possible as a wolf does. As he grows older, his ability to think and to stare down other animals makes him a leader in his jungle society. Although what he learns from the wolves and from Baloo, a bear, keeps him from

Mowgli's adventures take place in India.

developing human flaws such as greed, Mowgli's inborn human qualities make him a creature apart from the others.

Baloo. This brown bear is the wise master who teaches all animals the Law of the Jungle. He is an affectionate teacher to Mowgli, but he also sternly disciplines the animals when he feels they need to behave better.

Bagheera. The black panther is Mowgli's close friend. Bagheera was born in captivity, so he has a better understanding than any other jungle animal of the way humans think. In fact, Bagheera understands humans even better than Mowgli himself.

Shere Khan. The tiger Shere Khan was born lame in one foot. He often breaks the Law of the Jungle by killing humans and by hunting outside his own territory. Not only does he act unlawfully, he also often advises others to do the same.

Tabaqui. No other animal likes or respects Tabaqui the jackal, because he is completely untrustworthy and given to fits of insanity. [*See also* JUST SO STORIES by Rudyard Kipling.]

Justin and the Best Biscuits in the World

❖ Mildred Pitts Walter, 1986, contemporary realistic fiction, Coretta Scott King Award. Ten-year-old **Justin** goes to visit his grandfather's ranch. There he learns some fascinating facts about African American history. He also learns some important lessons in life. For example, Justin, who lives with his mother and sisters, loves basketball and hates household chores, which he thinks of as "women's work." When he goes to visit Grandpa Ward on his ranch, he finds that Grandpa does "women's work" all the time, including cleaning, cooking, and making the best biscuits in the world. When the visit is over, Justin's attitude toward his mother and sisters has improved

Just So Stories
❖ Rudyard Kipling, 1902, humorous fiction. These comic stories supposedly explain the origin of human activities, such as letter-writing, and of the unusual physical traits of some animals,

Author's Anecdote

Rudyard Kipling, author of THE JUNGLE BOOK and JUST SO STORIES, was born in India. He lived there until he was five. Then he was sent to England for several unhappy years. Returning to India at 16, he remained for a while, working as a journalist and developing his talent as a writer. Much of his work, including *The Jungle Book*, reflects his love for India.

An illustration from "How the Camel Got His Hump"

such as the camel's hump, the elephant's trunk, and the leopard's spots. For example, the author says that, once upon a time, elephants had no trunks. The first elephant to develop a trunk is **the elephant's child,** a young animal whose curiosity often gets him into trouble. One day, he gets too close to a hungry **crocodile,** who grabs the elephant's child by his short nose. The young elephant escapes with his life . . . and a much longer nose, which turns out to be quite useful. [*See also* THE JUNGLE BOOK by Rudyard Kipling.]

King of the Wind ❖ Marguerite Henry, 1948, historical/period fiction, Newbery Medal. The Sultan has ordered Agba, the Moroccan stable boy, to care for a young horse named Sham, which means "sun," from its birth to its death. Agba's travels with Sham take him from Morocco to France and then to England, where both horse and boy suffer one misfortune after the other until their luck finally changes.

Agba. The stable boy is mute, meaning he cannot speak. As a result, Agba does not easily have close human relationships. But he is faithful and devoted to Sham, the horse he loves so dearly. He promises the motherless colt that he will be a "father" to him and that Sham will grow up to be "King of the Wind," admired by all. The loyal Agba never goes back on his promise.

Mistress Cockburn. Agba meets a good-natured housekeeper in England. Mistress Cockburn takes pleasure in feeding and mothering Agba. When she finds that he has unjustly been thrown into jail, she visits him there.

Earl of Godolphin. Mistress Cockburn arranges for Agba's release by the earl. He is a kindly English nobleman who has fallen on hard times. After he frees Agba from prison, he buys Sham. His good deed is rewarded because one of Sham's colts eventually wins an important horse race, so the earl receives the money he needs to save his property. [*See also* MISTY OF CHINCOTEAGUE by Marguerite Henry.]

Last Summer with Maizon ❖ Jacqueline Woodson, 1990, contemporary realistic fiction, ALA Best Book for Young Adults. Margaret, an 11-year-old African American girl, suffers two painful events: her father's death and the departure of her best friend, Maizon, for an exclusive private school. With Maizon gone, Margaret's Brooklyn neighborhood turns bleak, and Margaret wonders whether she will ever be happy again.

Margaret. Quiet, shy Margaret is happy to live in Maizon's shadow. When Maizon leaves, Margaret discovers new inner resources. She finds that she is a gifted poet when she wins a citywide prize. She makes new friends and realizes that people change over time.

Maizon. Maizon is Margaret's inseparable friend until Maizon goes off to exclusive Blue Hill Academy. (Another book by Woodson is titled *Maizon at Blue Hill.*) Intelligent and self-confident, Maizon is not always as considerate as a friend should be. She sometimes does not fully appreciate Margaret's difficulties. After an unpleasant experience at the private school, Maizon begins to understand her own limitations and realize that there is more to Margaret than she had been aware of.

The Lion, the Witch and the Wardrobe ❖ C. S. Lewis, 1950, fantasy/science fiction/imaginative fiction. Four English children move to a country house, and the youngest, Lucy, sneaks into a wardrobe, which is a tall piece of furniture that is used as a closet. While exploring, she finds that the wardrobe leads her to a magical kingdom called Narnia. Later, her sister and brothers follow her there. In Narnia, they find all sorts of marvels and dangers, including talking animals and the wicked White Witch.

Aslan the lion and friends in the magical land of Narnia

The children search through Narnia for a noble Lion, who, they hear, is vital to the kingdom's happiness. This book is part of a series called the Chronicles of Narnia.

Peter. Lucy's 13-year-old brother, Peter, sees himself as a protector. Honest enough to apologize for doubting that Narnia is real at first, he goes on to become a heroic figure in the kingdom. To emphasize his nobility, he receives a real shield and sword. He is the most rational of the children and questions not only the reality of Narnia but a number of extraordinary events there that his reason says are impossible.

Susan. Lucy's practical 12-year-old sister, Susan makes the children wear fur coats in Narnia, since it is likely to be cold. She is fearful about undertaking challenges that appear risky. She is also apt to say, "I told you so" when events meet her pessimistic expectations.

Edmund. In many ways, Edmund, ten, is the opposite of Lucy. Where she is willing to trust her faith and instincts, Edmund demands proof of all claims before he will believe them. He is susceptible enough to temptation to be taken in by the White Witch's promise of candy, and he becomes her temporary ally. He later sees the error of his ways.

Lucy. Only eight when she finds Narnia, Lucy is the most innocent of the children. She is considerate of others and always ready to forgive anyone who repents having done something wrong. Lucy can be very brave in supporting her beliefs.

Aslan. Aslan is an enormous gold-colored lion who represents the power of good over evil. All the virtuous inhabitants of Narnia love and honor Aslan, while the evil ones hate and fear him. Though powerful, Aslan can be gentle and kind but tolerates neither dishonesty nor wickedness.

Jada, the White Witch. The White Witch claims to be Queen of Narnia. She sees herself as superior to other people, whom she considers subject to her wishes. As long as she controls Narnia, the kingdom is locked in eternal winter and gloom.

Little House on the Prairie

❖ Laura Ingalls Wilder, 1935, historical/period fiction. This book describes a family's life on the frontier in the 1860s, in what was then Indian Territory and is now Kansas. Indians play a significant role in the lives of these new settlers. Seeing the newcomers as intruders on their land, the Indians sometimes appear hostile. In the course of the book, the Ingalls family builds a house and a barn, begins to farm their land, gives and receives help from neighbors, and battles natural threats such as prairie fires and wolves. This book is one of a series based on the author's actual experiences as a child and young woman. In this book, as in many books based on fact, the main events actually happened, but many of the details are fictional (made up by the author).

Laura Ingalls. Young Laura often envies her older sister, Mary, for her curly, blond hair and for the praise Mary gets for her good behavior. Laura herself tends to be irresponsible and to get into trouble for impulsive conduct. But Laura is basically a good and kindhearted child who is always honest and is normally kind and considerate of others.

Pa Ingalls. Laura's father is a stern but loving parent whose word is final on all major family decisions. He is the one who chooses to move to Kansas. Then, even though he thinks

the area is too crowded, he is willing to stay there so that his children, whom he deeply loves, can get a proper education. He is a good neighbor and a tireless worker who is well suited to frontier life, where people must rely on their own skills and resources.

Ma Ingalls. Although Laura's mother seems to accept all of her husband's decisions, she somehow manages to get her way in many respects. It is she who first says that she wants the family to stay where the children can go to school. She expects her daughters to behave in a ladylike fashion and to observe the proper rules of etiquette for girls and women. She is a good housekeeper who makes her children's clothing, helps out with the farm chores, and is usually levelheaded and calm. Perhaps her most unattractive quality is her hatred of Indians.

Mary Ingalls. Mary is a year older than her sister Laura and quite different both in appearance and personality. Most people see Mary as the prettier child, and her meek and obedient attitude contrasts sharply with Laura's headstrong, rebellious nature.

Author's Anecdote

Laura Ingalls Wilder, author of LITTLE HOUSE ON THE PRAIRIE and several other books about frontier life in nineteenth-century America, wrote about the life she herself knew. This book and most of her other books were about her and her family's own experiences. The names of the Ingalls family in these books are the actual names of her family members. She wrote the books later in her life, using her childhood for their plots.

The Little Mermaid ❖

Hans Christian Andersen, 1828, fantasy/science fiction/imaginative fiction. This book is about both the beauty and the pain of falling in love.

The little mermaid in the sea, her natural home.

The story raises questions such as "How much will you give up for the one you love?"

The Little Mermaid. This creature of the sea saves a handsome prince from a shipwreck. She then hides from him, so he never knows to whom he owes his life. But the mermaid has fallen in love with the prince. In order to marry him, she must take on human form. So she visits the sea witch, who changes her mermaid's tail into two legs. Then she cuts out the mermaid's tongue as the terrible price for the transformation.

When the mermaid finds the prince, she learns that he is about to marry a beautiful princess. The rest of the story focuses on the mermaid's efforts to win the prince and on the heartbreaking choice she has to make.

The Prince. A good and kind young man, the prince treats the little mermaid as a beloved child. Because she cannot speak, he never knows how much she loves him.

A popular and critically acclaimed Disney film version of *The Little Mermaid* is available on videotape.

The Little Prince ❖ Antoine de St. Exupéry, 1943, fantasy/science fiction/imaginative fiction. While repairing his airplane after crashing in the Sahara Desert, an **aviator** meets a mysterious **little prince,** a young boy who seems to have come from nowhere. The prince says that he came from an asteroid where he was the only person. He tells the pilot of his journeys to six other asteroids, each inhabited by one adult. The prince asks many questions about life on Earth, and the man answers them as best he can. The pilot feels protective and loving toward the strange little boy. But the little prince remains a puzzle, giving no information about who he is or how he got to Earth. Though he has gained wisdom from adults, he keeps his childhood innocence. It is his innocent quality that touches the heart of the aviator.

Little Women ❖ Louisa May Alcott, 1868, historical/period fiction. During the Civil War, the March family faces severe challenges, at home and on the battlefield. Mr. March is a chaplain serving with the Union army, and his wife and four daughters must manage without him. Inspired by his letters, they decide to improve themselves and make do despite limited means. The author also wrote sequels to *Little Women*.

Margaret (Meg). The oldest March sister, 16-year-old Meg works as a governess, or tutor, to help support the family. She is pretty and vain about her looks. At one point, she indulges herself with a glamorous gown and a flirtatious manner, but she tries hard to overcome her vanity and dislike of work.

Josephine (Jo). At 15, Jo loves to read and wants to be a writer. Frustrated by the limitations placed on women by nineteenth-century society, she purposely behaves in ways thought of as unfeminine. She pays little attention to her appearance or clothes. Jo sees her primary character defects as pride and a quick temper, which she resolves to defeat.

Elizabeth (Beth). At 13, Beth is quiet, spending time with her dolls because she is shy with people other than her immediate family. However, she is capable of tenderness with people who are ill and can give them attentive care. She is also a gifted musician.

Amy. The youngest March sister, 12 years old, is spoiled and self-centered. She sometimes treats other people maliciously and has occasional tantrums. Amy does make a serious effort to reform.

Mrs. March ("Marmee"). Marmee is an ideal mother; she is loving, strict when necessary, but always ready with forgiveness and understanding for her daughters. Lack of money forces her to become an efficient, thrifty homemaker and to train her children to follow her example.

Mr. March. Though Mr. March appears only briefly in this book, his influence is great. After all, it is his letters that inspire the rest of the family. He is generous to a fault. In fact, in helping a needy friend, he has lost much of the family money.

Laurie Laurence. Laurie, 16, has been raised mostly by James Laurence, his wealthy grandfather. A friend of the Marches, Laurie is handsome and good-natured. He can be stubborn and would like to be a musician, to his grandfather's dismay.

James Laurence. Mr. Laurence is a wealthy man, whose crusty outward show masks a warm and kindly nature. He is stubborn and has broken off ties with his son, who has married a woman of whom the older man disapproves.

Lyddie ❖ Katherine Paterson, 1991, historical/period fiction, ALA Best Book for Young Adults, New York Times Notable Book. The book takes place in the 1840s and begins in Vermont. Mattie Worthen, abandoned by her husband, sends her children, Lyddie and Charlie, to work in order to pay family debts. Lyddie goes to work at a tavern, but, rather than accept cruel treatment, she goes to Lowell, Massachusetts, to work as a factory girl in a textile mill. There, inspired and taught by Diana, a new friend, Lyddie sees that she can seek a better life.

Lyddie Worthen. Lyddie is uneducated but intelligent and has the courage to refuse to tolerate abuse at the tavern. Under Diana's influence, Lyddie recognizes the injustices that the workers around her suffer and decides to set higher goals for herself.

Diana. Lyddie's friend Diana is a radical who helps Lyddie learn to read and appreciate the hard life of poor working people who are treated

Lyddie takes place in New England in the nineteenth century.

unjustly in places like the mill. When Diana, who is not married, becomes pregnant, she boldly goes elsewhere to make a life for herself and her baby.

Luke Stevens. Luke is a gentle young man who proposes marriage to Lyddie. Lyddie sees him as a person she could love, and she hopes he will wait for her until she has completed her studies. [*See also* BRIDGE TO TERABITHIA and THE GREAT GILLY HOPKINS by Katherine Paterson.]

The Magic School Bus: Inside the Earth ❖

Joanna Cole and Bruce Degen (illustrator), 1987, fantasy/science fiction/imaginative fiction, Boston Globe–Horn Book Honor Book. The teacher Ms. Frizzle starts off by telling her students that their next science topic is going to be rocks . . . and ends up taking them on one of her famous "field trips"—to the center of the Earth. How do they get there? On the magic school bus, of course! As in all the books in the Magic School Bus series, the kids end up learning much more than they would in a classroom.

Ms. Frizzle. This teacher is hardly usual, and her field trips are far from ordinary. To begin with, Ms. Frizzle dresses for her job, meaning that, in this book, her dress has pictures of pickaxes all over it, and her earrings are tiny shovels. But mainly, "the Friz," as her students sometimes call her, believes in learning by doing. And with a magic bus at her disposal, she is always ready to take her class on a field trip—even to such strange places as the center of the Earth. Her sense of humor helps to brighten her class's educational experiences.

Phoebe, Dorothy Ann ("DA"), and Arnold. These are Ms. Frizzle's most notable students. Phoebe has recently come from another school, where teaching and learning were carried out in the usual way. She has

The Magic School Bus makes learning a real adventure.

not yet gotten used to Ms. Frizzle's unusual teaching methods, and she often remarks that "they" did things differently "in my other school." Dorothy Ann is a bit of a know-it-all. She really does know a lot about everything, it seems, and she likes to give lectures that begin with the words, "According to my research . . . ."

Arnold is the biggest challenge. He is not always interested in science, and he is often less than enthusiastic about the field trips. For example, when Ms. Frizzle asks the class, "Don't you often wonder what is inside the Earth?" Arnold thinks to himself, "Not often." And instead of bringing a real rock to class, he brings a dirty piece of Styrofoam.

Maniac Magee ❖ Jerry Spinelli, 1990, fantasy/science fiction/imaginative fiction, ALA Best Book for Young Adults, Newbery Medal, Boston Globe–Horn Book Award. Orphaned at three, Jeffrey Magee escapes an unhappy life with his quarreling aunt and uncle and appears one day, nine years later, as a 12-year-old in Twin Mills, Pennsylvania, a town torn by tension between white and black people. His astonishing athletic skills make him a hero to local children, who nickname him "Maniac." Magee reaches out to people on both sides of the town's racial barrier, and his actions affect residents of all ages and ethnic groups.

Maniac Magee. Unaware of racial prejudice himself, Maniac can establish ties in the white and African American communities—though he meets with resistance at first. His athletic talent is awesome in every sport. Even as he opens the eyes of Twin Mills citizens to the foolishness of their bigotry, he remains an orphan who desperately wants a loving home.

"Mars Bar" Thompson. "Mars Bar" is a tough, streetwise ghetto boy, whose harsh treatment by white racists makes him hostile to whites in general. However, he is capable of changing his views when shown that his own attitude is biased.

Earl Grayson. Grayson, a one-time baseball player, becomes friendly with Maniac, who gets Grayson to open up and talk to Maniac about his life in sports. Maniac also helps Grayson overcome racial stereotypes based on ignorance.

Marvin Redpost: Kidnapped at Birth?

❖ Louis Sachar, 1992, humorous fiction. When Marvin Redpost learns that the King of Shampoon is searching for his son, who was kidnapped as a baby, Marvin decides that he was kidnapped at birth and that he is the long-lost prince. After all, the prince and Marvin are the same age, and both have red hair and blue eyes! The author has written other books featuring Marvin Redpost.

Marvin Redpost. This character is a well-behaved nine-year-old with a very active imagination that sometimes complicates his life. For instance, having decided that he is the missing Prince of Shampoon, Marvin tells his parents that they are not his real parents after all. He persuades classmates to bow to him and treat him like royalty.

Jacob Redpost. At 11, Jacob, Marvin's brother, realizes that Marvin can get carried away by wild ideas. He loves his brother and finds Marvin's imagination amusing rather than annoying.

Linzy Redpost. Only four, Marvin's little sister accepts whatever Marvin says as true.

Mr. Redpost. Marvin's father is patient with his son. He is slightly eccentric. For example, because of his last name, he has painted one post of the fence around his house red.

Mrs. Redpost. Mrs. Redpost shares her husband's amusement in Marvin's offbeat ways. [*See also* HOLES and WAYSIDE SCHOOL IS FALLING DOWN by Louis Sachar.]

Mary Poppins

❖ P. L. Travers, 1934, fantasy/science fiction/ imaginative fiction. Mr. and Mrs. Banks need a nanny to care for their four children. Suddenly, a remarkable woman drops from the sky—or floats down, using her umbrella like a parachute—and takes the job. She is Mary Poppins. The small carpetbag that is her only luggage seems to hold an endless supply of possessions; her single, small medicine bottle contains whatever kind of medicine a child might need, in any flavor. Mary Poppins not only cares for the children but also takes them on a series of magical adventures not only in this book but also in sequels.

Mary Poppins. Nobody calls this character "Mary" or "Miss Poppins." Everyone always calls her "Mary Poppins." She is a tidy, efficient nanny who performs her chores perfectly. She can be impatient with children and adults and is easily offended. She refuses to discuss her origins or produce references from past employers. She has a seemingly infinite supply of knowledge of every kind and appears to know everyone wherever she and the children travel. While she insists that she has no supernatural connections, she can talk to animals and use her umbrella as a sail, to let the wind carry her wherever she wants to go.

Jane. The oldest of the Banks children, Jane is the most observant member of the family, making her the person who deals best with Mary Poppins's frequent mood changes.

Michael. The second child, Michael tends to act impulsively, or in a rash manner, and is constantly curious about everything. His emotions sometimes run wild, and he can act destructively.

John and Barbara. The Banks's baby twins are young enough to still have the powers that human beings seem to lose as they grow older. It appears that John and Barbara can still talk to animals and still understand nature automatically, without someone else explaining it to them.

McBroom Tells the Truth

❖ Sid Fleischman, 1966, humorous fiction. Josh McBroom tells the tale—which sounds very much like a *tall* tale—of the one-acre farm he was tricked into buying from his dishonest neighbor. The land turns out to be under water. However, the soil is so rich that the McBroom family is soon harvesting three or four crops every day! The plot centers on the neighbor's efforts to steal back the farm and the McBrooms' fight to keep it.

Josh McBroom. The main character is a typical teller of tall tales, whose stories—including this one—are larger than life. But McBroom insists that every word he says is the absolute truth. His story, as well as his style of telling it, shows that he is optimistic and creative, and also proud of himself for having those qualities.

The underwater farm in *McBroom Tells the Truth* seems incredible.

Hector Jones. This is the cheat who sold McBroom the farm. Once he finds out how profitable the land really is, he lives only to get the farm back. [*See also* THE WHIPPING BOY by Sid Fleischman.]

M.C. Higgins the Great

❖ Virginia Hamilton, 1974, contemporary realistic fiction, ALA Best Book for Young Adults, Newbery Medal, Boston Globe–Horn Book Award, National Book Award. M.C. (Mayo Cornelius) Higgins, a 13-year-old African American boy, thinks his family should abandon their house before a huge mound of uprooted trees and dirt from an abandoned mine slides down and kills them all.

M. C. Higgins. Proud and self-confident, M. C. thinks that he can do anything and that he is always right.

Author's Anecdote

Virginia Hamilton comes from a family of great storytellers. Her maternal grandfather was born into slavery but escaped into a free state. Virginia, who was named for the state of her grandfather's birth, has vivid memories of his tales of life as a slave. Most of her writing deals with the lives of African Americans in the United States, past and present.

He even believes that he is old enough and responsible enough to replace his father as head of the family. M.C.'s experiences with a friend, Lurhetta Outlaw, teach him to be more humble, more sensitive, and more realistic about life.

Jones Higgins. M.C.'s father values tradition, so he refuses to abandon his home. He loves and respects his son but resents M.C.'s challenges to his authority. Although Jones is a good man, he has prejudice toward his neighbors, the Killburns. He thinks they are "witchy" because they have unusual skin and hair color and twelve fingers and toes instead of ten. Nevertheless, when M.C. makes friends with the Killburns, Jones changes his attitude.

Lurhetta Outlaw. Lurhetta makes M.C. understand that his father's attitude toward the Killburns is wrong. She teaches M.C. that he should think for himself rather than accepting whatever he is told. [*See also* THE HOUSE OF DIES DREAR and ZEELY by Virginia Hamilton.]

Merlin and the Dragons

❖ Jane Yolen, 1995, fantasy/science fiction/imaginative fiction. This is one of many stories about Arthur of Britain, a legendary character whose origins go back over a thousand years. In this version, the young king cannot sleep because he worries about shouldering the responsibilities of kingship. He visits his teacher, the wizard Merlin, who tells him a story about a young fatherless boy who, long ago, matched wits with an evil and powerful magician. Hearing the story—and learning the identity of the boy in the story—helps Arthur to gain self-confidence—and to fall asleep.

Arthur. Arthur becomes a king at an early age, at a time when kings faced constant danger of revolt or treachery. He lacks self-confidence, in part because of his youth, but also because he has not been brought up to rule. Though he is intelligent, he has not yet developed the strong will a king needs to survive.

Merlin. The wizard is understanding and sympathetic to Arthur. In his wisdom, he knows the right story to tell the young king to help him gain confidence.

Emrys. The fatherless boy in Merlin's story is lonely and afraid at the beginning of the story. As he becomes aware of his own powers, he becomes a courageous and confident young man.

Vortigren. The evil magician in Merlin's story is a typical villain. He tries to destroy a boy in order to serve his own ambitions.

Mick Harte Was Here ❖

Barbara Park, 1995, contemporary realistic fiction. When young Mick Harte dies in a bicycle accident—he was not wearing a helmet—his older sister, Phoebe, has trouble coming to terms with the tragedy. Both Mr. and Mrs. Harte have problems coping with the loss and their feelings of responsibility.

Mick Harte. Mick is seen only in his sister's flashback descriptions. He was, in many ways, a typical younger brother, teasing Phoebe and enjoying pranks. He was headstrong and refused to wear his helmet because he thought it made him look geeky.

Phoebe Harte. Mick's big sister is observant, giving many details about him and the effect of his death on the family. She is painfully honest and makes a point of describing ways in which she or her parents may have helped to bring about the accident.

Mr. Harte. Mick's father has strong feelings of guilt for not making Mick wear his helmet. In trying to hide these feelings, he turns away

People have been telling tales about Merlin for ages and ages.

from his family at first. Eventually, he reaches out so that they can comfort each other.

Mrs. Harte. Mrs. Harte initially feels isolated in her grief but, like her husband, realizes that she can help heal herself by being closer to her family.

Missing May ❖ Cynthia Rylant, 1992, contemporary realistic fiction, ALA Best Book for Young Adults, Newbery Medal, Boston Globe-Horn Book Award. Summer is a 12-year-old orphan who has been living with her Uncle Ob and Aunt May in rural Appalachia. When Aunt May dies, Summer and Ob are devastated. Ob is still so affected six months after May's death that Summer fears for his life. When Ob says that May's spirit has visited him,

Author's Anecdote

Cynthia Rylant, author of *Missing May*, grew up in the Appalachian Mountains, where this book is set. Like Summer, young Cynthia lived for a time under the care of older relatives, her grandparents. Her grandfather's advice might easily have been something Aunt May would say: "Always do the best you can with what you've got."

Summer looks for help from spiritualists in contacting May again. Summer cares for Ob so deeply that, for a time, she cannot focus on her own feelings of loss.

Summer. Summer never knew love until Ob and May took her in. May's death, in addition to the fear of losing Ob, leaves Summer depressed and pessimistic. Before Summer can feel hopeful and loving again, she must go through a healing process and learn to cope with her grief.

Uncle Ob. Ob is a wounded World War II veteran, unable to work. Though Summer is not his daughter, he has loved her as he might have loved his own child. The loss of May overwhelms Ob at first, leaving him unable to feel any emotion other than misery for some time after May dies.

Aunt May. Though May is dead when the story opens, Summer's narrative shows May's love and warmth as a force in the home. May knew tragedy and loss, especially the untimely loss of her parents and her inability to bear children, but she was able to overcome these blows. Her death leaves Ob and Summer with an emotional emptiness in their lives. [*See also* HENRY AND MUDGE by Cynthia Rylant.]

Miss Rumphius ❖ Barbara Cooney, 1982, contemporary realistic fiction. **Miss Alice Rumphius**

Miss Rumphius

Story and Pictures by BARBARA COONEY

Books inspire Miss Rumphius to travel far and wide.

works as a librarian in an inland city and is determined to see the colorful places she has read about. Because she has a strong will, she achieves her goal, traveling all over and making friends wherever she goes. Like her grandfather, an artist, Miss Rumphius also wants to make the world a more beautiful place, even though she lacks artistic gifts. Through hard work and persistence, Miss Rumphius overcomes her limitations. Her story is narrated by her great-niece, who shares her great-aunt's determination and wants to carry on Miss Rumphius's tradition some day.

Misty of Chincoteague

❖ Marguerite Henry, 1947, contemporary realistic fiction. Paul and Maureen Beebe live with their grandparents on Chincoteague Island, off the coast of Virginia. Every year, people from Chincoteague round up wild ponies from nearby Assateague and swim them across the bay between the two islands. Paul captures a mare (female horse) and her foal (baby horse). Paul and Maureen train the two horses, which they name Phantom and Misty, but they know that the older one, Phantom, longs to return to the wild herd on Assateague Island.

Paul and Maureen. Paul and Maureen show good sense and courage in facing the changes and dangers they must deal with. Both children love horses and are sensitive to the animals' feelings and needs.

Phantom and Misty. The mare never loses her wild nature, although she does run in a race and win. Misty, however, is easily tamed and has a sweet, lovable nature. [*See also* KING OF THE WIND by Marguerite Henry.]

Mop, Moondance, and the Nagasaki Knights

❖ Walter Dean Myers, 1992, contemporary realistic fiction. The Kennedys adopted T. J., Moondance, and Mop from the same orphanage. The three children play baseball for the Elks. New to the team is Greg, a homeless boy who lives in the park with his mother. The children want to help Greg but fear that he might be taken away from his mother if they try to do so. In the meantime, the Elks are about to compete in a baseball tournament with their rivals, the Eagles, and three foreign teams. The winners will get to play in Japan.

T. J. The narrator of the book is T. J. He is sometimes dishonest with both himself and the reader. He claims to be a better ballplayer than he is, partly because he wants his parents to be proud of him. But T. J. is likable, wants to be loved, and wants to do the right thing about Greg.

Moondance. The sensitive Moondance is terrified that Greg will be taken from his mother and become an orphan, as he once was. Although a talented pitcher, Moondance has to get over his fear of hitting a batter with the ball.

Mop. In the orphanage, Mop feared that no one would adopt her.

*Other Works by
Walter Dean Myers*

The Blues of Flats Brown
Fast Sam, Cool Clyde, and Stuff
The Glory Field
Hoops
Me, Mop, and the Moondance Kid
The Mouse Rap
The Outside Shot
Scorpions

She fights at the drop of a hat but is lovable in spite of her toughness.

Morning Girl ❖ Michael Dorris, 1992, historical/period fiction, New York Times Notable Book. As this book begins, in the year 1492, the Taino Indians are living peacefully on their beautiful Caribbean island. A brother and sister, Morning Girl and Star Boy, explore the natural world together. All is well on the island until the end of the book when Morning Girl, while taking a swim, sees a canoe full of white strangers who frighten her.

Morning Girl. As the reader can guess from her name, this 12-year-old loves the daytime and the sunlight. She rises before the rest of the family to enjoy the early morning. Since her people have no mirrors, she is frustrated at not knowing what she looks like, until she sees a reflection of herself in her father's eyes.

Star Boy. Morning Girl's younger brother loves the night and its mystery. While the rest of the family sleeps, he stays up to enjoy the darkness.

Other Taino Indians. The parents of Morning Girl and Star Boy love and accept their children for who they are. The Taino people are kind, trusting, and peaceful. Their world darkens when the Europeans appear in their three ships.

Mr. Popper's Penguins

❖ Richard Atwater and Florence Atwater, 1938, fantasy/science fiction/imaginative fiction. In the small town of Stillwater, Mr. and Mrs. Popper live with their two children. Mr. Popper is a housepainter who would rather be an Antarctic explorer. When he writes a letter to the explorer Admiral Drake, Drake sends him a gift—a penguin named Captain Cook. The Poppers adopt a second penguin, Greta, to keep Captain Cook company, and soon there is a family of penguins in the house.

Mr. Popper. An impractical dreamer, Mr. Popper longs for adventure in far-off places—especially the South Pole. First, he lets Captain Cook live in the refrigerator. Then, to make sure all his penguins are comfortable, he keeps the windows opened, even in winter, and turns the floor into an icy playground.

Mrs. Popper. An agreeable woman, Mrs. Popper puts up with the penguins, but she is much more practical and not nearly as imaginative or adventurous as her husband.

Penguins in their natural home, the Antarctic.

Mrs. Frisby and the Rats of NIMH

❖ Robert C. O'Brien, 1971, fantasy/science fiction/ imaginative fiction, Newbery Medal, Boston Globe–Horn Book Award. Mrs. Frisby, a field mouse, lives in a garden with her children. Her husband is dead. When a farmer's plow threatens her home, Jeremy, a crow rescued by Mrs. Frisby from a tangle of string, helps her. He advises her to consult some rats living under a nearby rosebush. The rats turn out to be very impressive. They are not only extremely strong, they are remarkably smart as well. They even have running water and electricity! Originally normal rats, they were trapped for an experiment run by the National Institute for Mental Health (NIMH), which resulted in their becoming highly intelligent; then they escaped. They treat Mrs. Frisby with special respect when they learn that she was married to Mr. Frisby, their close friend. Later, Mrs. Frisby learns that a scientist from

NIMH wants to kill the escaped rats, whom she must somehow warn and help.

Mrs. Frisby. Mrs. Frisby not only loves her family but cares for other creatures as well. For example, she rescues Jeremy, the crow, and runs risks to save the rats when they are endangered. She is also intelligent (for a field mouse) and can read a few words. Her bravery becomes heroism in this book.

Jonathan Frisby. Jonathan, Mrs. Frisby's late husband, was also part of a NIMH experiment that made him more intelligent. The rats respected him for his wisdom and bravery.

Mr. Ages. Mr. Ages is another field mouse who, like Jonathan Frisby, was genetically altered at NIMH. He lives alone, makes herbal medicines, and gives Mrs. Frisby valuable advice.

Nicodemus. Nicodemus is the dignified leader of the rats of NIMH. Thoughtful and wise, he dreams of founding an enlightened community for his followers. Nicodemus admires human accomplishments but has reservations about human science and technology.

Justin. Justin is a good-looking NIMH rat who was responsible for planning the escape of the rats from the laboratory.

Jeremy. The crow, Jeremy, whom Mrs. Frisby rescued, is not very bright; he gets tangled up in string and is not clever enough to get loose. But he is grateful to Mrs. Frisby and remains a loyal ally.

Dr. Schultz. Dr. Schultz is an ambitious scientist who works for NIMH. He regards all nonhuman creatures as lesser beings not worthy of kindness or consideration. He thinks that he can use and discard them as he pleases.

From the Critics

Mrs. Frisby and the Rats of NIMH is popular with readers of all ages. One reader writes:

> This story has long been one of my favorites and deserves to be a (future) classic. O'Brien introduces many serious issues into his fascinating tale. . . . O'Brien reminds us of the dangers of genetic tampering and points out the similarities between rats and the human species when it comes to issues such as self-sacrifice, courage, faith, and hope.

Mrs. Piggle-Wiggle ❖

Betty MacDonald, 1947, fantasy/science fiction/imaginative fiction.

Mrs. Piggle-Wiggle lives in a house where everything is upside down—except for the kitchen, bathroom, and stairs. She is very popular with neighborhood children. They love to come for tea and cookies and to dig in Mrs. Piggle-Wiggle's garden for the treasure Mr. Piggle-Wiggle buried there when he was a pirate.

Mrs. Piggle-Wiggle. Mrs. Piggle-Wiggle's most remarkable quality is her special talent for curing childhood diseases. Parents come to her for the "Won't-Pick-up-Toys Cure," the "Fighter-Quarrelers Cure," the "Bad-Table-Manners Cure," and others. The cures are very odd. For instance, bad table manners are cured by a large, very polite pig named Lester, who teaches by setting a good example. Mrs. Piggle-Wiggle earns the children's love by listening carefully to their fears and concerns and by being warm, loving, and caring herself.

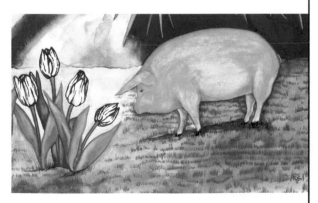

A polite pig teaches children good manners.

My Daniel ❖ Pam Conrad, 1989, contemporary realistic fiction, ALA Best Book for Young Adults. Twelve-year-old Julia Creath lives on a farm in nineteenth-century Nebraska. She loves her brother, Daniel, and his sudden death leaves her grief-stricken. Long afterward, Julia, now an 80-year-old grandmother, takes her grandchildren to New York's Museum of Natural History, where she reveals a secret that she has kept since childhood.

Julia Creath. Life on the farm is grim for Julia. Her only joy is her brother Daniel's companionship, and she never fully recovers from his loss, even though she grows up to marry and have a family. As an adult, she seems neither warm nor affectionate; her deepest emotional ties are still those to her brother, who is her fondest and most important memory.

Daniel. When Daniel, four years older than Julia, first learns about fossils and dinosaurs, he develops a passion for these relics of a long-dead age. He is determined to find the remains of a dinosaur on his farm. Despite his interest in dinosaurs, Daniel is proud to be a farmer and wants to remain on the family land. He turns down an offer to go exploring with a party of dinosaur hunters. Daniel hopes that finding a dinosaur will bring financial rewards so that he can help pay the mortgage on the farm and buy his family a few expensive gifts.

My Side of the Mountain ❖ Jean Craighead George,

1959, contemporary realistic fiction, Newbery Honor Book. Tired of city life, teenager Sam Gribley decides to live alone in the wilderness, in an isolated part of New York State's Catskill Mountains. He builds a home in a tree and befriends several wild animals, including a baby falcon, a weasel he rescues from a trap, and a raccoon. He learns to provide for his daily needs and encounters occasional human visitors.

Sam Gribley. Sam is tough and determined. Although he makes mistakes from inexperience early on, he learns from them and does not get discouraged. Sam has great love and respect for nature. Eventually, he comes to place a higher value on human contact as well.

Bando. Bando admires Sam for his beliefs. He teaches Sam about important people who shared Sam's viewpoint about nature and civiliza-

Sam Gribley and the falcon he trains in the wilderness.

tion. One of these people was the philosopher Thoreau.

Matt Spell. Though this young would-be journalist is inexperienced and naive, he is intelligent enough to grasp Sam's ideas. Spending time with Sam in the wilderness makes Matt more appreciative of the wonders and beauties of nature. [*See also* JULIE OF THE WOLVES by Jean Craighead George.]

Narnia ❖ *See* THE LION, THE WITCH AND THE WARDROBE.

Nate the Great ❖ Marjorie Weinman Sharmat, 1972, mystery. When Annie calls on her friend **Nate the Great**, boy detective, to find a picture that she drew of her dog, Nate is hot on the trail. Nate has been given the nickname "The Great" because of his detecting skills. His specialty is finding lost items for his friends. While he is on the job, he does not talk much and never eats—not even pancakes, his favorite food. He prefers action to conversation and thinks of each new case as a fascinating challenge. With persistence, determination, and, most of all, careful observation, Nate knows he can crack any case. The author has written other books about Nate's cases.

Nightbirds on Nantucket ❖ *See* THE WOLVES OF WILLOUGHBY CHASE.

No Such Thing as a Witch ❖ Ruth Chew, 1971, fantasy/science fiction/imaginative fiction. A newcomer arrives in the Coopers' Brooklyn, New York, neighborhood. Her name is Maggie, and she turns out to be a witch!

Maggie Brown. Maggie is a good witch—a strange, giggly old lady who loves animals and has a special gift for communicating with them. Her powers involve a special recipe for fudge, which causes a person to like animals, understand what they are saying, or even *become* an animal. Her love for animals gets her into trouble with the landlady, who claims that she keeps too many animals in the apartment.

Nora Cooper. Nora Cooper is the cautious older sister of the Cooper family, who tries to protect her little brother, Tad. Nora is suspicious of Maggie at first but eventually helps the witch out when Maggie's landlady says that Maggie has too many animals in her apartment.

Tad Cooper. This character, Nora's younger brother, has a strong sense of adventure. He is daring, rushes into things without thinking, and sometimes gets into trouble—

especially when he eats too much of Maggie's fudge.

Number the Stars ❖ Lois Lowry, 1989, contemporary realistic fiction, Newbery Medal. The story is set in Denmark when the German Nazis took control of it during World War II. The Nazis were killing millions of Jews in Europe. The heroic actions of the Danish people saved most of Denmark's Jewish population.

Annemarie Johansen. At ten, Annemarie believes herself to be a coward because she is frightened by the German occupation forces. At the same time, Annemarie is terrified about what might happen to her close friend Ellen Rosen if the Germans learn that Ellen is Jewish. Like many other Danes, Annemarie decides that she will take whatever risks are necessary to keep Ellen alive and out of the hands of the Nazis. She discovers that a true hero acts bravely despite fear and that, often, heroic acts are impulsive, or sudden, rather than planned. For example, Annemarie impulsively rips a Star of David from around Ellen's neck before the Nazis notice the incriminating item. In addition, Annemarie discovers that she is capable of quick-witted deception and improvisation.

Ellen Rosen. Annemarie's Jewish friend Ellen is an imaginative and creative girl who brings out the best qualities in Annemarie.

Inge Johansen. Inge, Annemarie's mother, is a woman of strong will and character. Like her daughter, she is willing to take great risks to save her Jewish friends from death. Her courage shows when she breaks her ankle. She fights the pain and crawls unaided for hours to reach Annemarie and calm her anxiety.

Uncle Henrik. Annemarie's uncle is a fisherman who lives on the coast and helps smuggle Jews out of Denmark into neutral Sweden. He also provides Annemarie with wise advice on the nature of heroism. He tells her that the bravest people are those who act despite their fear. He goes on to explain to her that good people are obliged to fight evil for the public welfare.

Peter Nielsen. At the beginning of the book, Peter is a fun-loving free spirit. After the Nazis kill his fiancée, he becomes a dedicated member of the Danish Resistance, which fights the Germans. Until she discovers her own strength, Annemarie sees Peter as the kind of hero that she believes she could never be. [*See also* ANASTASIA KRUPNIK and THE GIVER by Lois Lowry.]

Old Yeller ❖ Fred Gipson, 1956, historical/period fiction, Newbery Honor Book. In Texas in the 1860s, young Travis Coates must be "the man of the house" while Papa goes on a cattle drive. With Papa

Old Yeller goes from stray to friend.

away, Travis's young brother Little Arliss adopts a stray dog and names him Old Yeller. Although Travis dislikes the dog at first, he comes to love Old Yellar.

Travis Coates. At 14, Travis must grow up quickly when his father leaves. He takes his responsibilities seriously. Initially, he resents his mother and brother for not respecting him enough. Travis has trouble coming to terms with sorrow and is harsh on what he sees as his failings. Still, Travis faces several challenges to his bravery and honor, which toughen and mature him.

Old Yeller. A missing ear indicates that Old Yeller's early life must have been harsh. He must have lived by his wits for some time and is a clever thief, stealing meat on occasion. But once he feels that he is part of the Coates family, he will risk his life for their safety.

Papa. Though absent for much of the book, Papa has a strong influence on Travis. He teaches Travis to accept what is unavoidable in life, even when it is unpleasant.

Orphan Train Series ❖
See A FAMILY APART.

Out of the Dust ❖
Karen Hesse, 1997, contemporary realistic fiction, Newbery Medal. This story is set in Oklahoma during the Depression, a time of hardship in the 1930s. Life was particularly difficult for farmers in the part of the state known as the Dust Bowl, where the ground was dry from lack of rain. The reader learns about the plot, the theme of survival, and the main character's feelings through poems written by that character.

Billie Jo. This character is the person who writes the free-verse poems that make up the book. She is 14 and 15 in the course of the story and is the only character whom the reader gets to know very well.

Billie Jo is a pianist who is dreaming of a musical career. Her world turns upside down when her mother, pregnant with a son, dies after being badly burned by an accidental fire in which both Billie Jo's father and Billie Jo had some part. In addition to losing her mother and her brother in the fire, Billie Jo has severely burnt her hands.

Somehow, Billie Jo finds the strength to write poetry even when she cannot play the piano, her relationship with her father falls apart, and the horror of losing her mother pains her greatly. She forces herself to enter a contest and, in spite of the awful pain from her burned hands, manages to win third prize for her piano playing.

As more time passes, Billie Jo feels she must give up the piano and her home. She thinks that only if she leaves the area, only if she can get "out of the dust," will she be able to survive. She makes the break, leav-

They survive, but Billie Jo and her father feel the effects of the fire.

ing town on a freight train. Next, she learns an unexpected lesson, and she—and the reader—can see that life may improve.

Billie Jo's father. The father drinks heavily as his wife lies dying. His grief, like Billie Jo's, is very deep, but the father is not able to talk or to reach out to his daughter for a long time after the tragedy. Finally, though, after the contest, he tells her she "did him proud." Eventually, Billie Jo comes to describe her mother as being like the tumbleweed, which holds on but then must blow away, and her father as being like Billie Jo herself, "more like the sod / Steady, silent, and deep."

Oz ❖ *See* THE WONDERFUL WIZARD OF OZ.

The Peterkin Papers ❖ Lucretia P. Hale, 1880, humorous fiction. Because they do not have an ounce of common sense among them, the Peterkin family, who live in a village near Boston, have comical adventures all the time.

Mrs. Peterkin. The wife is easily scared and easily confused. When she gets confused, a simple problem can grow into a huge and complicated one.

Mr. Peterkin. The husband, Mr. Peterkin, cannot see the obvious solution to the simplest problem.

Agamemnon. The Peterkins' son, Agamemnon, has not yet graduated from college, although he has been to five of them. He tries to help the family solve problems by making totally ridiculous suggestions.

Elizabeth. Elizabeth, the Peterkins' daughter, is a good-hearted girl, but she can never make up her mind about anything and has a terrible memory.

The Lady from Philadelphia. The Peterkins' neighbor is the only character in the book with common sense. She always shows up in the nick of time to give them good advice and solve their problems.

Peter Pan and Wendy ❖

Sir James Matthew Barrie, 1921, fantasy/science fiction/imaginative fiction. One night, while Mr. and Mrs. George Darling are out, their children—Wendy, John, and Michael—have unexpected visitors: Peter Pan, a magical boy, and his fairy companion, Tinker Bell. Peter is able to fly and has determined to remain a child forever rather than grow up. He persuades the Darling children to fly with him to Neverland, where he lives. There, he says, they can join the Lost Boys, some children who have lived in Neverland since falling out of their baby carriages.

Peter Pan. By remaining a child forever, Peter can avoid all the burdens adults must take on. However, he will always be immature and impulsive, sometimes putting

Peter convices his new friends to fly with him to Neverland.

the lives of his friends at risk. Lacking an adult's sense of responsibility, Peter does not realize how selfish he is. He is vain and touchy about being the leader of the Lost Boys and is seldom grateful for the help of others, even when they risk their lives to save his. His faults are offset by an attractive personality that serves him well as a natural leader.

Wendy Darling. The oldest Darling child, Wendy becomes a substitute mother for other Neverland children. Because she has strong maternal instincts, she does not mind this role. She enforces rules about going to bed at the proper time. She also has domestic skills, sewing Peter's shadow back on when he loses it. Unlike Peter,

Wendy does not fear becoming an adult some day.

John Darling. The middle Darling child is the braver of the brothers. He likes to wear a hat, which represents his greater maturity.

Michael Darling. The youngest Darling child is treated like a baby much of the time, but he is loyal to Peter even when threatened by Captain Hook.

Tinker Bell. Tinker Bell is a tiny fairy who is jealous of Peter's affection for Wendy. Her loyalty toward Peter is so great that she drinks poison meant for him, risking her own death.

Captain Hook. The pirate captain is an elegant villain with long, curly hair. He has a hook at the end of his right arm to take the place of the hand he lost to the crocodile. Sneaky, lying, and cruel, Hook fears nothing except the crocodile that bit off his hand.

Nana. Nana is a huge Newfoundland dog whom the Darling parents use as a nurse for their children. She is the one who rips off Peter's shadow when he takes the Darling children away to Neverland.

Peter Pan was originally a play, written by Barrie in 1904, which has been popular ever since. It has been adapted into a musical that is often performed on stage and is also the basis for an animated motion picture.

The Phantom Tollbooth

❖ Norton Juster, 1961, fantasy/science fiction/imaginative fiction. **Milo** receives a small tollbooth as a gift. When he sets it up and drives past it in his toy car, he finds himself in a magical place—the Land Beyond. Guided by a flying dog, he meets a whole cast of strange characters. Two of them, the Mathemagician and King Azaz, give him the difficult task of rescuing the princesses Sweet Rhyme and Pure Reason and returning them to the Kingdom of Wisdom. At the beginning of the book, Milo is bored with everything and thinks that learning is useless and a waste of time. He returns from his adventures looking at things in a new light, eager to explore everything that life has to offer.

Pippi Longstocking ❖

Astrid Lindgren, 1945, fantasy/science fiction/imaginative fiction. Pippi Longstocking is an orphan who lives by herself with a white horse and a monkey named Mr. Nilsson. She leads her friends Tommy and Annika in one adventure after another.

Pippi Longstocking. The central character of this book is unusual in appearance, habits, and personality. Her two bright orange braids stick straight out from her head, and she wears long stockings, one black and one brown, with gigantic black shoes. She sleeps with her head

Pippi Longstocking may look unusual, but she is dependable.

under the covers and her feet on the pillow. Pippi is so strong that she can lift her horse down from the porch when she wants to ride him. Independent, imaginative, and not afraid of anything, Pippi shows her well-behaved friends, whose parents do not approve of her, how to have fun. Pippi proves her intelligence and resourcefulness when she figures out how to save two children from a burning house. The same character is featured in several sequels.

Poppy ❖ Avi, 1995, fantasy/science fiction/imaginative fiction, Boston Globe–Horn Book Award. Poppy, a deer mouse, lives with her family near Dimwood Forest, where they are in perpetual fear of Mr. Ocax, a fierce horned owl. This self-proclaimed king of the forest demands total obedience from the mice. Lungwort, the oldest mouse, insists that all the mice obey the owl, who protects them from attack by fierce porcupines—or so Mr. Ocax says. Poppy, however, has her doubts and decides to see if the owl's claims are true.

Poppy. Like most animals who are preyed on by others, Poppy is fearful and cautious. Her determination to explore unknown territory and to face unknown dangers is, therefore, a sign that she is brave. She is observant and intelligent in dealing with Mr. Ocax and the other unfamiliar and potentially deadly creatures she meets.

Lungwort. Lungwort, the patriarch, or head, of the deer mice, dreads the idea of change; he prefers to accept Mr. Ocax's tyranny rather than rock the boat. Lungwort has survived to old age not because he is wise but because he is timid.

Mr. Ocax. The big horned owl bullies weaker animals, but, despite this fierce behavior, he is neither as powerful nor as intelligent as he wants the mice to think he is.

Rabbit Hill ❖ Robert Lawson, 1944, fantasy/science fiction/imaginative fiction, Newbery Medal.

Rabbit Hill is a very special place to the animals that live there.

Food has been scarce on Rabbit Hill, and the animals who live there hope that the New Folks who move into the house will plant a garden. But the animals worry that the New Folks may not be friendly to them.

Little Georgie. This daring young rabbit goes on a challenging journey to bring a wise old rabbit, Uncle Analdus, to Rabbit Hill. Georgie's enthusiasm and optimism, along with his strength, help him complete the journey successfully.

Uncle Analdus. This character is wise and experienced, but his pessimism and distrust cause the other animals to fear that the New Folks are evil before they get to know them.

Father and Mother Rabbit. He is wise and considerate and a loving father to Georgie. She is a worrier.

The New Folks. The Man and the Lady are gentle and kind. They appreciate nature and do all they can to live peacefully with the animals in their garden and the surrounding fields. [*See also* BEN AND ME by Robert Lawson.]

Ramona Quimby, Age Eight ❖ Beverly Cleary, 1981, contemporary realistic fiction. Ramona Quimby has to deal with some big changes. She is going to a new school and has to take a bus. In addition, her parents both have jobs now, so she has to go to the Kemps' house every day after school. Many of Ramona's attempts to be a successful eight-year-old are funny, but to Ramona, being eight is not easy.

Ramona Quimby. The main character is the youngest member of the Quimby family. Sometimes she feels that she is treated unfairly because she is the youngest. Like many children her age, she sometimes shows off, misbehaves both at school and at home, and is stubborn. At times, she also feels sorry for herself, especially when she is sick and does not think she is getting enough sympathy. On the other hand, Ramona is imaginative and creative, as shown in her unusual book report.

Beezus Quimby. This character, whose real name is Beatrice, plays only a small role in this book. She finds Ramona to be an annoying, pesty little sister. Still, Beezus sticks up for Ramona when anyone outside the family criticizes her.

Willa Jean Kemp. Willa Jean is a four-year-old who annoys Ramona by constantly demanding attention and always wanting her own way

Author's Anecdote

Beverly Cleary was born Beverly Atlee Bunn on April 12, 1916, in McMinnville, Oregon. She spent her early years on a farm but grew up in Portland, Oregon. Later, she graduated from the University of California, Berkeley, married Clarence Cleary, and became a children's librarian. She published her first book, HENRY HUGGINS, in 1950.

Beverly Cleary said:

> . . . I had had enough of [reading] books about wealthy English children who had nannies and pony carts or books about poor children whose problems were solved by a long-lost rich relative turning up in the last chapter. I wanted to read funny stories about the sort of children I know, and I decided that some day when I grew up I would write them.

when Ramona goes to the Kemps' house after school.

Danny. Ramona calls Danny, one of the children in her class, "Yard Ape" because he acts bratty and rude and steals her eraser. But Danny later shows himself to be a basically nice person. [*See also* DEAR MR. HENSHAW; HENRY HUGGINS; and RUNAWAY RALPH by Beverly Cleary.]

Rascal ❖ Sterling North, 1963, memoir. This book tells about true events that took place when the author was growing up in a small town in Wisconsin. Sterling lives with his father, who is away from home often. To keep busy, Sterling builds a canoe in the living room and has many pets, including Poe-the-Crow and Rascal, the young raccoon Sterling captures and tames.

Rascal. The raccoon gets himself—and Sterling—into one amusing mess after another. Rascal is smart and mischievous. He rides in Sterling's bike basket, eats in a high chair, gets into the neighbors' vegetable gardens, and steals a diamond ring from Sterling's sister. Finally, Sterling has to face the possibility that Rascal may need his freedom.

Sterling. For an 11-year-old boy, Sterling is unusually independent, perhaps because he is left on his own more than most boys his age. He loves animals and has a deep appreciation for nature.

Redwall ❖ Brian Jacques, 1986, fantasy/science fiction/imaginative fiction. The mice of Redwall Abbey have enjoyed peace for years. Now an army of rats and other vermin, led by the savage Cluny, plans to attack and enslave Redwall.

Matthias. Humble Matthias does not see himself as the stuff of

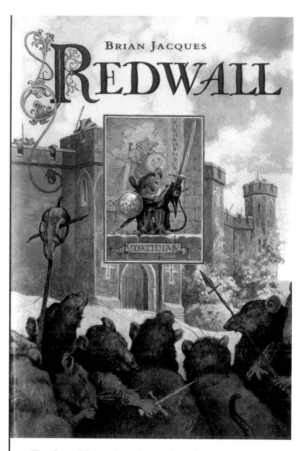

Redwall is the first book in a bestselling series.

which heroes are made; he is too apt to stumble over his own feet.

Abbot Mortimer. Wise old Mortimer, the abbey's leader, is a gentle mouse who detests violence. Such an attitude puts him at a disadvantage in this crisis.

Cluny. This huge, one-eyed rat terrifies even his allies. He wants to be a tyrant and is cunning enough to put on a soothing manner when it suits him, but he is merciless.

Methuselah. Methuselah is the oldest and wisest of the abbey mice.

He alone sees Matthias's heroic potential.

Constance. Constance is a powerful badger who is a valuable friend of the Redwall mice. She is crude but clever and a fearsome enemy to those she dislikes—like Cluny's army.

Rescue Josh McGuire ❖

Ben Mikaelsen, 1991, contemporary realistic fiction. Josh McGuire, 13, has had a hard time since his older brother, Tye, died. Not only does Josh miss Tye, but Josh's father, Sam, has changed. Now Sam drinks too much and treats his wife and son badly. When Sam kills a female bear while hunting, Josh rescues the bear's cub. Unable to accept his father's cruelty any longer, he runs away with the cub. Sam tries to put his family together again, but it will take a lot for Josh to forgive Sam.

Josh McGuire. This character's emotions are at war with one another. Josh both loves and hates his father; he misses his older brother but is still competing with him. Then Josh gains the courage to stand up to his father and finds, when he is on his own, that he is as capable, courageous, and resourceful as Tye was.

Sam. Josh's father, Sam, knows he risks losing his family because of his behavior. He makes up his mind to stop drinking and become, once again, the good father he was before.

The Rescuers ❖

Margery Sharp, 1959, fantasy/science fiction/imaginative fiction. Miss Bianca lives a life of ease and is an unlikely candidate for a rescue mission. But the story deals with a job that requires a mouse who speaks Norwegian, and she becomes part of a team with Nils, a seagoing mouse. They encounter some risks, most significantly a nasty cat named Mamelouk.

Miss Bianca. This character is a pet who lives a luxurious life in an elegant porcelain house, eating fine food and wearing a silver chain around her neck. Though intelligent and creative—she writes poetry—she is ignorant of the hazards of the outside world. She is not even aware that a cat, given the chance, will eat mice! But once she learns about such perils, she proves resourceful.

Bernard. A lowly pantry mouse, Bernard loves Miss Bianca, though she is unaware of his feelings. He involves her in the rescue and, not wanting to frighten her, avoids mentioning Mamelouk. By withholding information about the cat, Bernard actually increases the danger to Miss Bianca. In a crisis, Bernard is loyal.

Nils. This rough, fearless seafarer is an indispensable team member. He finds the escape route.

Mamelouk. The large black cat enjoys torturing potential victims before killing them. He is also very stupid, and Miss Bianca takes advantage of his stupidity.

Roll of Thunder, Hear My Cry ❖ Mildred D. Taylor, 1976,

contemporary realistic fiction, ALA Best of the Best, Coretta Scott King Award, Newbery Medal, Boston Globe–Horn Book Award. The story takes place in Mississippi during the 1930s. The Logans are an African American family struggling to make a living from their land. They cope with racial bigotry in many forms.

Cassie Logan. Nine-year-old Cassie, who narrates this story, is a tough fourth-grader. She does not accept being treated as a second-class citizen. Consequently, she often gets into battles that she cannot win in the Mississippi of the 1930s. A bright girl, she is a good judge of character and believes in speaking her mind.

Stacey Logan. Cassie's teen-aged brother Stacey shares her resentment of racial discrimination. As he approaches adulthood, he is conscious of needing to take on more responsibility, so he sees himself as the protector of his younger siblings.

Christopher-John Logan. This is Cassie's seven-year-old brother, a quiet and easy-going boy who prefers to avoid trouble and confrontation. When faced with tense situations, he becomes increasingly timid.

Clayton Chester ("Little Man") Logan. This six-year-old is the youngest Logan sibling. He becomes frustrated and angry when faced with racism, even though he cannot always explain his feelings..

David Logan. The head of the Logan family is a hard-working, loving father. He is proud of his heritage and willing to fight for what he believes is right. At the same time, he understands the world well enough not to endanger his family by being too outspoken.

Mary Logan. Cassie's mother is much like her husband, industrious

Racial bigotry is at the center of *Roll of Thunder, Hear My Cry.*

From the Critics

Readers of *Roll of Thunder, Hear My Cry* often studied the book in school. One such reader writes:

> This is one of the best books I have ever read about racism. It shows you how lucky we are today to have equal rights. I would recommend this book to people who love to read. I couldn't give it a higher score or I would have.

and proud. She teaches in a local school and dislikes seeing other teachers act in an overly polite manner toward white people. She is a strict teacher who treats all her students alike—even her own children.

T. J. Avery. Stacey's friend T. J. is an unintelligent and underhanded boy who creates serious problems for Mrs. Logan when he blames her for his poor school record. Being slow-minded, T. J. is fooled by people who want to take advantage of him.

Runaway Ralph ❖ Beverly Cleary, 1970, fantasy/science fiction/imaginative fiction. Ralph is a mouse who lives with his mouse family at Mountain View Inn. Looking for ex-citement, he runs away on his toy motorcycle to Happy Acres Camp. But one of the campers catches him, and Ralph ends up in a cage. When he discovers that he can communicate with Garf, the boy who caught him, Ralph hatches a plan. Garf has been wrongfully accused of stealing a girl's watch. Ralph will help Garf prove his innocence. In return, Garf will set Ralph free.

Ralph. Unlike his timid relatives, Ralph needs speed, thrills, and adventure. Even his nighttime motorcycle races through the halls of the inn do not provide enough excitement. Ralph shows independence and courage by going to Happy Acres. There, he proves himself to be not only intelligent but also daring and resourceful. He outwits a cat named Catso. He also masterminds the plan that will clear Garf of suspicion and regain Ralph's freedom. In that way, Ralph can get back to the inn—where life is pretty good, after all.

Garf. Grouchy Garf does not get along with the other campers. He is also selfish. When he finds that Ralph can talk and ride a motorcycle, he still plans to keep Ralph as a pet rather than let him loose. Only when Ralph delivers on his promise to prove Garf's innocence does Garf hold up his side of the bargain. [*See also* DEAR MR. HENSHAW; HENRY HUGGINS; and RAMONA QUIMBY, AGE EIGHT by Beverly Cleary.]

Sarah, Plain and Tall

❖ Patricia MacLachlan, 1985, historical/period fiction, Newbery Medal, New York Times Notable Book. Jacob Witting, a widowed farmer living in the American Midwest during pioneer days, advertises for a wife to share his life and to be a mother to his children, Anna and Caleb. Sarah Wheatley writes from her home in Maine and agrees to a trial visit. The children are eager for a mother but fear that she might not want to stay.

Sarah. The main character, who describes herself as "plain and tall," is ready to leave her family home. Her strong maternal feelings help her to fit in immediately with Anna and Caleb. Sarah shows her love of fun by sliding down hay piles; she shows her energy by learning farm skills such as driving a wagon. Though she misses her former home, she compensates by drawing pictures of what she left behind.

Papa Jacob Witting. This character is a hardworking, loving father. He misses a wife's companionship and tries hard to accommodate Sarah.

Anna. As the older child, Anna bears the burden of caring for her brother and doing the household chores. She deeply feels the absence of a mother.

Caleb. Inquisitive and observant, Caleb constantly tries to figure out whether Sarah will stay or leave.

The Secret Garden ❖

Frances Hodgson Burnett, 1911, historical/period fiction. After the disease cholera kills the rest of her family in India, young Mary Lennox goes to live with her uncle, Archibald Craven, in England. In the old family manor, the girl is neglected by her uncle and most of the household staff. She is unhappy and bored. Then Mary learns from a servant about a mysterious garden on the grounds. The uncle closed off the garden after the death of his wife. Mary becomes curious about this garden and its history. In searching out its secrets, she

Caring for the garden helps Mary, Colin, and others to be happy.

makes further discoveries about the house, the family, and herself.

Mary Lennox. A lifetime of neglect has left young Mary sickly and disagreeable. Once she develops ties of affection in her uncle's household and focuses on the garden, Mary becomes physically stronger and emotionally more caring. Her concern for the garden causes her to enlist the help of others, leading to new friendships. It becomes clear that Mary's negative qualities were a product of the indifference of those around her.

Colin Craven. Mary's cousin, like Mary, is frail and moody. He, too, has felt neglect. For most of his life, the boy has been a "nonperson" in his home, left to his own resources. Thanks to his constant reading, Colin is highly imaginative. Once he joins Mary in caring for the garden, he becomes stronger and more assertive. This causes his father to see him in a new light.

Archibald Craven. Mary's uncle suffers from a physical deformity:

From the Critics

Generations of readers of *The Secret Garden* have loved this book and introduced it to their children. One reader writes:

> I read this as a child and adored it. Last year I read it to my then 7-year-old daughter. It has absolutely wonderful lyrical prose which makes it a joy and a delight to read out loud as I did. The theme of love and transformation is so soul nourishing.

he is a hunchback. He has also renounced all the pleasures of life since the death of his wife. Because his wife's once-beautiful garden reminds him of her, he has closed it off until it is barren and overgrown with weeds. His coldness extends even to his son Colin.

Martha Sowerby. This is the person who looks after Mary's daily needs in the Craven home. Cheerful and high-spirited, she is the one who first tells Mary about the garden. By forcing Mary to dress and groom herself, Martha begins the process of making the girl independent.

Shadow of a Bull ❖

Maria Wojciechowska, 1975, contemporary realistic fiction, Newbery Medal. Because **Manolo Olivar** is the son of a great bullfighter, everyone in his hometown expects Manolo to become one too. However, from the age of nine, Manolo has believed that he is a coward, afraid to fight bulls. He is torn: he fears the bulls but fears admitting cowardice even more. Manolo envies an older boy, **Juan García,** whose ambition to be a bullfighter is matched by his bravery. Finally, when Manolo meets a wise bullfighting critic, Alfonso Castillo, the boy learns that it is sometimes more courageous to ignore public pressure and follow one's dream.

Shiloh ❖

Phyllis Reynolds Naylor, 1997, contemporary realistic fiction, Newbery Medal. Set in a town named Friendly, West Virginia, this story has a simple plot but a complicated theme. The plot involves saving a dog. The theme involves asking hard questions such as, Is it ever all right to lie?

Marty Preston. This 11-year old, who tells the story, loves the outdoors and animals. When he makes friends with a dog that has been beaten, the boy faces a choice between lying and truth telling. Marty has promised the owner to turn over the dog if he finds him. However, he cannot bring himself to return the dog to the mean man, so he hides the dog, which he names Shiloh.

Finally, Marty must face the dog owner and stand up for the dog and for himself. Once he starts bravely talking back to the owner, he hears himself saying, "So what are you going to do? Shoot me?" He and the owner work out a deal that will allow Marty to keep Shiloh. But Marty still worries about doing the right thing. Does making the deal put other animals in danger and mean Marty is no better than the owner?

Judd Travers. Marty gives the reader several reasons for disliking the dog's owner, Judd Travers: the man cheats a store owner, spits tobacco, blocks Marty's view at the fair, and kills deer out of season. Worst of all, Travers mistreats dogs.

Dad. Marty's father is furious when he learns Marty has been hiding the dog, but he puts his anger aside in order to take Shiloh, hurt by another dog, to Doc Murphy. With time, Dad, like Marty's sisters and mother, grows to love Shiloh. He lets Shiloh lick his dinner plate clean, removes a tick, and says, ". . . there's food for the body and food for the spirit. And Shiloh sure enough feeds our spirit."

The Sign of the Beaver

❖ Elizabeth George Speare, 1983, historical/period fiction, Newbery Honor Book. The story is set in colonial America in the 1760s. Young Matt stays alone in his new Massachusetts home while his father goes to fetch the rest of the family. The 13-year-old has to fend for himself for weeks, a difficult task in a rugged, isolated region. His problems grow when a thief steals his rifle, leaving him neither protection nor a way to hunt. When Matt meets two Indians—a grandfather and a grandson—he is unsure of their intentions. But the grandfather helps him and asks him to teach Attean, his grandson, to read. Matt soon sees that Attean has more valuable lessons for him than he has for Attean.

Matt. Matt is resourceful enough to live alone in the wild and perceptive enough to appreciate Attean's survival skills and use them. He also comes to respect Attean's beliefs and way of life.

Attean. The same age as Matt, Attean is scornful and suspicious of white people, who have given him reason to dislike them. But he gradually learns to respect Matt and regard him as a friend. He discovers that generalizations about any group of people can be misleading. [*See also* THE WITCH OF BLACKBIRD POND by Elizabeth George Speare.]

So Far from the Bamboo Grove

❖ Yoko Kawashima Watkins, 1986, memoir, ALA Notable Children's Book. This is the author's account of the ordeal she and her family went through in 1945, after World War II. Yoko's family had been part of the Japanese ruling class then living in Korea. These people controlled Korea until Japan's defeat in the war. Like many other Japanese, the family had to somehow find their way through Korea to reach Japan and safety.

Yoko Kawashima. Only 11 when her story begins, Yoko has never known hunger or danger. Early in this story, she acts spoiled. For example, she is unwilling to share food with others equally needy or to let her hair be cut even to protect herself. During her dangerous journey, hardship toughens her and brings out her bravery and determination.

Ko. Yoko's sister, a few years older, better understands the risks of the family's situation. She is often harsh with Yoko when the younger girl is selfish or weak. But she is devoted to her sister and mother, sacrificing her food for them and taking on humiliating tasks, like shining shoes, to provide them with a little money.

A Solitary Blue ❖ *See* DICEY'S SONG.

Sounder ❖ William H. Armstrong, 1969, historical/period fiction, Newbery Medal, New York Times Best Book for Young Readers. A poor African American man, struggling to feed his family in a time of racial injustice, steals some food. Deputies arrest him and shoot his dog, Sounder, when the dog defends the man. Wounded, the dog runs away. The man is sentenced to work on a chain gang, leaving his wife and son alone in a harsh and uncaring world.

The boy. At the beginning of the book, the son is a timid child. The brutal conditions of life bring out his willpower and desire to improve his life; one of his goals is to learn to read. Life tests the boy in many ways as he matures.

The father. The man is strong and honest. He resorts to theft only to keep his family from starvation. The inhuman conditions of his prison life cripple him emotionally and physically.

The mother. Powerful religious beliefs help the mother to cope with her difficult life. She is a tireless worker who encourages her son to persevere. She also fires his imagination with Bible stories.

The teacher. The wise, elderly teacher teaches the boy to read and

From the Critics

Readers of *Sounder* find the book moving and powerful, with a message for all ages. One reader writes:

Sounder is the story of a boy's journey to manhood, about the importance of family, education, and compassion. Written simply and with truest humanity, it is a book that reaches both children and philosophers alike. (I'm not surprised it is read in schools throughout the world.)

also educates him in the ways of the world.

Sounder. The father's hunting dog is deeply loyal. He is determined to survive his wounds and see his master again.

This story was made into a movie in 1972.

Soup ❖ Robert Newton Peck, 1974, memoir.

In this book, the author writes of his experiences as a boy named Rob growing up in rural Vermont in the 1930s. Sometimes the stories deal with the typical mischief of small boys. Sometimes the stories involve more serious matters—for example, confessing to misbehavior and facing punishment. The author has written several sequels that follow Rob as he grows up.

Robert Peck ("Rob"). A third-grader in this book, Rob sometimes tries to avoid the consequences of being naughty or other misbehavior, but he is usually honest enough to admit that he is guilty. He admires his best friend, Soup, and generally follows Soup's lead. Often, Rob tries to test himself by taking on challenges that demand bravery or maturity.

Luther Wesley Vinson ("Soup"). Soup hates his given name and is willing to fight any boy who calls him "Luther." Imaginative and impulsive, Soup gets ideas that often lead Rob and himself into trouble. Because he is slightly older than Rob, Soup sees himself as the smarter and more authoritative of the two. He is a considerate friend who looks after Rob when Rob needs help and is ready to console his friend when Rob is unhappy.

Stolen Lake ❖ *See* THE WOLVES OF WILLOUGHBY CHASE.

Stone Fox ❖ John Reynolds Gardiner, 1980, historical period fiction, New York Times Notable Book.

It is some time before the age of cars and telephones. All seems hopeless on a Wyoming potato farm. Where will Grandfather and Young Willy get the money they need to hold onto the farm?

Willy. When Grandfather becomes ill, ten-year-old Willy refuses to move to someone else's home or sell the farm. He shows his strong

Author's Anecdote

Robert Newton Peck, the author of *Soup*, became familiar early on with farm life. He learned first-hand about raising, tending, and even slaughtering livestock, all of which are described in detail in his books.

Author's Anecdote

When John Reynolds Gardiner, author of *Stone Fox*, was 28, he started the Num Num Novelty Company, which sold plastic neckties filled with water and goldfish. His brother thought that anyone who had the imagination to dream up such a product should be a writer. He talked Gardiner into taking a television-writing class. Six years later, Gardiner had not sold a single TV script, but he sent a story about a boy and his dog to a book publisher. That story became the book *Stone Fox*.

will and his love for Grandfather by taking care of him, by planting and harvesting a potato crop himself, and by practicing hard for a dogsled race that offers a $500 prize—enough money to save the farm.

Grandfather. Readers learn that Grandfather is a wonderful, warm-hearted person as Willy remembers playing and working with him in better days. Clearly, Grandfather believes in hard work, education, and self-reliance.

Stone Fox. A Shoshone Indian, Stone Fox seems to have a name that fits. He is hard and silent, like a stone. Willy is in awe of Stone Fox but can stand up to him. Stone Fox's final act in the book shows that, in spite of appearances, the Indian understands and respects Willy.

The Story of Doctor Dolittle, Being the History of His Peculiar Life

❖ Hugh Lofting, 1920, fantasy/science fiction/imaginative fiction, Newbery Medal. Doctor John Dolittle's collection of pets grows so huge that his human patients leave him. After his parrot, Polynesia, teaches him animal languages, Doctor Dolittle develops a successful veterinary practice. He becomes famous and travels all over the world.

Doctor John Dolittle. Doctor Dolittle has good intentions but is impractical. Since he cares little about money, he often cannot meet his expenses. He is reluctant to turn away any animal—even a crocodile. He also believes that animals should be allowed their freedom. His caring and kindly nature makes him popular with children as well as animals.

Polynesia. Almost two hundred years old, Polynesia, Doctor Dolittle's pet parrot, speaks animal and human languages and loves human slang expressions. She enjoys pointing out when humans display ignorance or foolishness.

A parrot helps Doctor Dolittle with his medical practice.

Chee-Chee. This character is a monkey whom Doctor Dolittle rescues from an abusive street musician. Chee-Chee becomes a useful guide to the doctor in his travels.

The Story of the Treasure Seekers ❖ E. Nesbit, 1899, historical/period fiction. The six children of Richard Bastable try to rebuild the family fortune, lost through the dishonesty of Mr. Bastable's business partner. Their efforts fail repeatedly, but they keep planning new schemes.

Dora Bastable. Dora, the oldest child, seems trapped between childhood and adulthood. Her mother, on her deathbed, told Dora to care for her brothers and sisters, a responsibility that weighs heavily on her. Based on books she has read, she suggests that the children dig for buried treasure.

Oswald. Twelve-year-old Oswald, the narrator, loves books by Rudyard Kipling (see THE JUNGLE BOOK and JUST SO STORIES) and Arthur Conan Doyle. Sometimes he confuses the real and the make-believe. Then he sees himself as a hero from romantic fiction.

Dicky. Careful, practical Dicky never acts on impulse. He is the most likely one to raise realistic objections to schemes.

Noel. Delicate in health, Noel writes poetry and expects to marry a princess some day.

Alice. Noel's twin sister, Alice, is a tomboy who loves to play with the boys and worries about Noel's health.

Horatius Octavius. The youngest Bastable is headstrong and often impolite because he lacks education.

Stuart Little

❖ E. B. White, 1945, fantasy/science fiction/imaginative fiction. Stuart Little is a mouse. At birth, he is only about two inches tall. The interesting thing is that Stuart's older brother, George, and his parents are human beings.

Most of Stuart's adventures are based on either the advantages or the problems of being very small. Additional adventures are based on Stuart's love for a beautiful bird named Margalo.

Stuart Little. In spite of his size, Stuart is amazingly self-reliant and independent. He is also intelligent, brave, resourceful, and sophisticated. Stuart demonstrates these qualities by managing to take a bus by himself, using a tool to turn on the faucets in the sink, and saving Margalo from capture by a cat. Perhaps Stuart's most important characteristic is his determination to follow his dream, which is to find his beloved Margalo when she flies away.

Frederick C. Little and Mrs. Little. Stuart's parents love their son and try to make his life as pleasant as possible. Not surprisingly, they tend to be overprotective at times. [*See also* CHARLOTTE'S WEB by E. B. White.]

Summer of the Swans

❖ Betsy Byars, 1970, contemporary realistic fiction, Newbery Medal. Since their mother died, Sara, her sister, and her mentally handicapped brother have lived with their aunt.

Swans from the setting of this book, which is about much more than swans.

The book covers two days, during which Sara takes Charlie to a lake to see swans, Charlie gets lost, and Sara participates in a search to find him.

Sara Godfrey. Fourteen-year-old Sara has many problems. She thinks she is unimportant and unattractive, she is sick of taking care of Charlie, she finds her aunt annoying, and she resents her father, who is hardly ever home and who has become sad and gloomy. Two experiences help Sara change. First, Sara, who holds grudges and never admits she is wrong, apologizes to a boy named Joe for falsely accusing him of stealing Charlie's watch. Second, searching for Charlie makes Sara aware that she loves her brother. Sara begins to feel better about herself and gains a deeper understanding of her father's sadness.

Charlie. Charlie is ten years old and has not spoken since he was three. He gets confused easily, but his excitement about the swans shows that he loves and appreciates beauty.

Wanda. Sara's 19-year-old sister is pretty but, unlike Sara, believes that looks are not important. She helps Sara to have faith that things will get better for her some day.

Through the Looking Glass ❖ *See* ALICE'S ADVENTURES IN WONDERLAND.

Treasure Island ❖ Robert Louis Stevenson, 1882, historical/period fiction. In a room in the inn owned by his father, who has recently died, Jim Hawkins finds a map showing where a treasure is buried. Jim shows the map to the wealthy Squire Trelawney, who hires a ship to sail to the island where the treasure is buried. Trelawney signs on Captain Smollett and a crew, including Jim and a one-legged ship's cook named Long John Silver. Little does Jim know that Silver and other crew members are really pirates who plot to mutiny, kill Trelawney and Smollett, and keep the treasure for themselves. Soon a boy's romantic dream turns into a nightmare, complete with violence and even murder. Jim finds himself playing an important part in deciding the outcome of the voyage.

Jim Hawkins. Fourteen-year-old Jim is a sensitive boy who dreams of adventure. Jim, though, is immature and a poor judge of character. Because Long John Silver is charming and well dressed, Jim cannot believe he is a pirate. Rather, Jim admires Silver because Silver shows the boy special attention. On the

This illustration is from an early edition of *Treasure Island*.

other hand, Jim dislikes Captain Smollett, a good man, because Smollett does not approve of favoritism and pays no more attention to Jim than to the other crew members.

Jim's best qualities are bravery and a sense of honor. When he learns of the planned mutiny, he fights against the pirates. When captured by them, he refuses to escape because he has given his word that he will not. What really saves Jim from disaster, though, is luck.

Long John Silver. The bold pirate is both the villain of the novel and its most charming character. Silver makes a dashing appearance. He is handsome, tall, strong, and well dressed. He is also intelligent and witty and has a winning smile. All these qualities enable Silver to talk people into doing what he wants. On the other hand, he is dishonest and greedy.

The Pirates. The pirates aboard the ship are a rough and villainous bunch. They drink too much rum, swear constantly, and never seem to wash. One is uglier and more scarred than the next.

Author's Anecdote

Robert Louis Stevenson, the famous Scottish author of adventure novels such as *Treasure Island* and *Kidnapped*, began his life as a sickly child who loved to read. Like Jim Hawkins, the young Stevenson dreamed of adventure. As an adult, Stevenson's health improved, and his dream of adventure came true.

Several years after writing *Treasure Island*, Stevenson sailed a yacht to the South Seas with his wife, mother, and stepson. For the next six years, he explored the area and then settled on one of the islands of Samoa. The islanders liked Stevenson so much that they built a road to his house and called it The Road of the Loving Heart. When Stevenson died in 1894 at the age of 44, local chiefs buried him on top of a mountain.

Tuck Everlasting ❖ Natalie Babbitt, 1975, fantasy/science fiction/imaginative fiction, ALA Notable Children's Book. In August of the year 1880, Winnie Foster goes into the woods and discovers Jesse Tuck, a teenage boy. He is drinking water from a spring at the base of a tree. Later, when Jesse takes her home, Winnie learns that the spring is a secret, magic one. People who drink from it will never die. They will never even age, become ill, or get injured. All the people in Jesse's family—his father, mother, and brother—have drunk from the spring, but they are not happy. Eternal life, they explain to Winnie, is not necessarily a blessing. Death is an important part of life, they say—perhaps the part of life that makes living so wonderful. Winnie is not sure she agrees, but she helps the Tucks in their desperate fight to stop a man who has found out the secret of the spring from selling its waters.

Winnie Foster. As a result of growing up in an overprotective home, Winnie has a hard time making friends. Other children think of her as too prissy, neat, and meek to be any fun. In the relaxed atmosphere at the Tucks' home, Winnie learns to be more comfortable with people. She also develops the courage to take tremendous risks in order to help the Tucks protect the secret of the spring. She becomes more assertive and independent and gains the maturity to make the most important decision of her life— whether or not to drink from the spring herself.

Angus Tuck. Jesse's father drank from the spring when he was already older, and he is now tired of living. He is sad most of the time and smiles only when he is dreaming about death. Angus explains to Winnie why death is so important for a happy life.

Mae Tuck. Jesse's mother also believes that eternal life is more a curse than a blessing, but she does not complain as much as her husband.

Miles Tuck. Jesse's older brother is stuck at the age of 22. He is bitter about what has happened to him and his family but is determined to do something useful.

Jesse Tuck. Seventeen-year-old Jesse is the only member of the Tuck family who is not unhappy. He thinks the purpose of life is to have fun and sees no reason why the fun should not go on forever. While the others in his family think that drinking the water from the spring would cause Winnie to be unhappy, Jesse encourages her to drink. He has fallen in love with Winnie and wants her to become immortal.

The Man in the Yellow Suit. The man who wants to get rich by selling the water from the spring is evil and greedy. He believes that money is the only important value in life.

War Comes to Willy Freeman

War Comes to Willy Freeman ❖ James Lincoln Collier and Christopher Collier, 1983, historical/period fiction. This novel covers the period 1781 to 1783. The American Revolution was coming to a close, and the young country was setting up its government.

Willy (Wilhelmina) Freeman. Life changes forever for Willy, a 13-year-old free black girl, when the British kill her father and take her mother as a prisoner to New York City. Willy disguises herself as a boy as she sets out to locate her mother. She cannot read or write, but Willy uses common sense and courage to survive.

Willy, who tells the whole story as a first-person narrator, shares her feelings very openly. For example, she admits her fears when she steals a boat and sails toward New York City. She thinks often about the lack of freedom that slaves and women suffer, and she comments frequently on her feelings about being free.

Jack Arabus. Willy's Uncle Jack is a slave who has earned his freedom by fighting in the war in the place of a white man, Captain Ivers. But Arabus is having trouble claiming his freedom from Ivers. Throughout, Arabus has hopes of starting a business, saving money, and then buying the freedom of his wife and child, who are still owned by Ivers. Arabus is wise. He knows whom to trust and passes on his knowledge to Willy.

Horace. Willy's uncle has told her to seek out Sam Fraunces, a tavern owner, in New York. As Willy approaches the city, she coincidentally meets Horace, a skinny young man, who works for Fraunces. Horace helps Willy, who he thinks is a boy, get a job with Fraunces and search for her mother. Horace talks a great deal, often telling stories in which he is the hero. He also knows—and teaches Willy—the best ways to lie for self-protection in dangerous times. When Horace learns that Willy is a girl, his behavior toward her changes.

War Comes to Willy Freeman is part of the saga of the Arabus family. Other titles are *Jump Ship to Freedom* and *Who Is Carrie?*

The Watsons Go to Birmingham–1963

❖ Christopher Paul Curtis, 1995, contemporary realistic fiction, ALA Best Book for Young Adults, Coretta Scott King Honor Book, Newbery Honor Book. During the winter of 1963, Kenny Watson's family drives from Flint, Michigan, south to visit Grandma in Birmingham, Alabama. The usual family antics keep the trip lively and amusing. The Watsons are headed toward one of the darkest moments in America's history—the church bombing that left four young African American girls dead.

Kenny Watson. Ten-year-old Kenny is an intelligent, well-behaved boy who loves his family but cannot help delighting in his older brother's mischief. The depth of Kenny's nature is clear from the grief and horror he feels after the bombing.

Byron Watson. "By," Kenny's 13-year-old brother, thinks he is cool. Byron's rebelliousness gets him in trouble with his parents, especially when he straightens and bleaches his hair. Yet Byron shows sensitivity and maturity by supporting Kenny through the painful, difficult period after the bombing. [*See also* BUD, NOT BUDDY by Christopher Paul Curtis.]

Wayside School Is Falling Down

❖ Louis Sachar, 1989, humorous fiction. Wayside School is strange. It is 30 stories tall with one room on a floor—and no elevator. The nineteenth floor is not there, and Miss Zarves, who teaches on the nineteenth floor, is not there either. But she has a class, anyway. If this sounds confusing, so is everything else about Wayside School. The author has written other books about Wayside.

Benjamin Nushmutt. Benjamin, a new student, finds everything at Wayside puzzling. Perhaps the biggest mystery is that everyone insists on calling him "Mark Miller."

Mrs. Jewls. This teacher teaches on the thirtieth floor. People who misbehave write their names on the blackboard. If they misbehave three times, they must go home. Mrs. Jewls sends herself home one day.

Miss Mush. This character runs the cafeteria—Miss Mush's Room—and students stay away from her lunches, especially Mushroom Surprise. The surprise is what happens to any student unwise enough to eat it. [See also HOLES and MARVIN REDPOST: KIDNAPPED AT BIRTH? by Louis Sachar.]

The Westing Game

❖ Ellen Raskin, 1978, mystery, Newbery Medal, Boston Globe–Horn Book Award. Sixteen people receive invitations to live in Sunset Towers. They also receive a challenge: they must compete to identify a murderer. The competitors pair off and are given clues to help them. The winner will inherit a fortune. As the competition continues, entrants make discoveries about the tenants' complex histories.

Samuel W. Westing. This character is an American success story— a poor immigrant who became rich and, therefore, loves America. He has had tragedy in his family; his daughter, who had been out of touch with him, died in a car accident. Westing enjoys disguising himself.

Jake Wexler. Middle-aged Jake claims to be a podiatrist, or foot doctor, but is really a gambler. He is bullied by his wife.

Sun Lin Hoo. Jake's partner learns English from him and develops a more assertive personality.

Turtle Wexler. Thirteen-year-old Turtle is not pretty, so her mother neglects her. Turtle is brilliant, with a flair for finance.

Flora Baumbach. Grandmotherly Flora develops a close bond with Turtle, giving her the support that her mother does not.

Christos Theodorakis. Christos is 15 and confined to a wheelchair. The game gives him his first real social life.

Dr. Denton Deere. This character, a young plastic surgeon, learns to appreciate life from his partner, Christos.

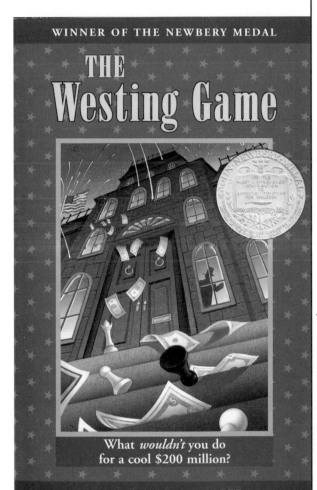

WINNER OF THE NEWBERY MEDAL

THE **Westing Game**

What *wouldn't* you do for a cool $200 million?

ELLEN RASKIN

The Westing Game turns out to be about more than just a game.

Where the Red Fern Grows ❖ Wilson Rawls, 1961, contemporary realistic fiction. This novel is based on the author's youth in the Ozarks in the early twentieth century. The Ozarks cover parts of Oklahoma, Arkansas, and Missouri. At the beginning, ten-year-old Billy Colman wants hunting dogs. The book shows Billy working for his dogs, gaining fame, dealing with sadness, and moving on.

Billy Colman. Adventurous Billy loves the wilds near his house. Billy demonstrates determination in whatever he undertakes.

When Billy gets the "dog-wanting disease" and his parents do not have money, he quietly saves every penny he needs for two years. Although he has never been to town, he walks there alone, barefoot, to get his dogs. He chops until he brings down a tree and hunts until the dogs find the trickiest game.

Later, another boy, named Rubin Pritchard, has an awful accident. Billy feels some responsibility for what happened, along with shock. Although he knows that it will be hard, he visits Mrs. Pritchard to talk about Rubin.

Finally, Billy has to part with his dogs and does what he must, as always. Then, just as the Colman family moves to town, Billy finds a positive way to look at his experiences.

Grandpa. This character has a twinkle in his eye and a special place for Billy in his heart. Grandpa knows when Billy needs candy, teaches him hunting tricks, and tells him about a championship coon hunt. Grandpa admits to Billy his own sense of guilt over Rubin's accident.

The Pritchard Boys. Nobody likes the Pritchards. Rubin and Rainie talk back to Grandpa and say bad things about him. They chew tobacco, try to act older, and tease Billy into making a bet.

The Whipping Boy ❖ Sid Fleischman, 1986, historical/period fiction, Newbery Medal. Prince Horace's constant misbehavior never leads to punishment—for *him.* Princes may not be whipped; instead the whippings go to Horace's whipping boy, Jemmy. When Horace runs away in search of excitement, he orders Jemmy to go with him. Unprepared for the world beyond the court, the boys experience its brutality, including capture.

Prince Horace. This character, also known as Prince Brat, gets into mischief because he is bored with his life. Used to having his way, he mistreats people; for example, when Jemmy plans to escape the bandits, the prince gives him away. However, as the prince experiences rough treatment himself, he finds unexpected strength and refuses to react to the pain of his first whipping. Horace begins to understand the responsibilities of a prince.

Jemmy. The orphan Jemmy has experienced the worst life has to offer without complaint. He is bright, learning to read and write by paying attention to lessons intended for the prince. Jemmy's sense of loyalty keeps him from abandoning Horace. [*See also* MCBROOM TELLS THE TRUTH by Sid Fleischman.]

White Fang

❖ Jack London, 1906, animal fiction. White Fang, part wolf and part dog, comes from the frozen Canadian north. He begins his life in a wolf pack and learns the first rule of wilderness survival: "Eat or be eaten."

White Fang. This animal grows into a powerful, crafty fighter who can dominate wolves and dogs. Though he regards all unfamiliar creatures as enemies, his dog instincts make him yield to humans. When a man treats him kindly, White Fang becomes loyal and protective.

White Fang examines the difference between dogs and wolves.

Kiche. This dog leaves her Indian master for a wolf pack, where she mates and then bears White Fang. She retains awe for her old master but still feels drawn to the pack.

Grey Beaver. This character is Kiche's master and, for a time, owns White Fang. Though he values White Fang highly, being kind to dogs is not in his nature.

Beauty Smith. This cowardly gambler enters White Fang in dogfights. White Fang endures only cruelty at his hands.

Scott Weedon. This young man from California frees White Fang from the gambler and is determined to win the animal over by humane treatment. [*See also* THE CALL OF THE WILD by Jack London.]

The Wind in the Willows

❖ Kenneth Grahame, 1908, fantasy/science fiction/imaginative fiction. Deciding he is tired of housecleaning, Mole abandons his underground home for the bank of the river, where he meets a new friend, Water Rat. Mole moves in with Rat and adopts Rat's leisurely way of life. Later on, Rat introduces Mole to a wealthy acquaintance, Toad of Toad Hall. While wandering in the woods, Mole and Rat look for shelter from a snowstorm and stumble on a new companion, Badger. The book contains stories about these and other animals.

Mole. Because this character has always lived in a small burrow, he thinks of his life as dull and unchanging. When he leaves his familiar surroundings, he enters an exciting but strange new world, and his lack of experience exposes him to dangers like snowstorms. Mole demonstrates poise and good sense in coping with his new environment and shows himself to be brave and quick-witted in helping his friends recover Toad Hall.

Finally, Mole discovers that, while he should avoid monotony, there is much to be said for a home's familiar surroundings. He learns that it is good to have roots.

Water Rat. Cheerful and outgoing, this character helps Mole learn to live around the water and is always ready to lend a hand in a crisis. He encourages Mole when his friend grows discouraged. At one point, Rat feels tempted to become a wanderer,

In this scene, Badger is saying, "Now then, follow me!"

but his friends, seeing potential danger in that choice, restrain him.

Toad of Toad Hall. This wealthy character is proud of his stately home and tends to be smug about what he sees as his high position in life. He tends to become obsessed with "fads," such as automobiles, and loses his common sense when in the grip of a new passion. He lets his friends take on jobs that he sees as tedious, but he does not show any appreciation. Despite these flaws, Toad is not mean, merely unaware of his faults. He is capable of generosity on occasion.

Author's Anecdote

Kenneth Grahame, the author of *The Wind in the Willows*, began his book as a story to tell his four-year-old son, Alistair, at bedtime. He later added to the original story in letters to Alistair while the boy was on vacation.

Badger. This character is not very sociable. He has a few friends but generally avoids company and uses a gruff outward manner to hide a tendency toward kindness. Badger feels protective toward Toad, and, because Badger is powerful and has a temper, other animals are unlikely to harm anyone under Badger's protection.

Winnie-the-Pooh ❖ A. A. Milne, 1926, fantasy/science fiction/imaginative fiction. This is a collection of stories told by a father to his little boy. The boy, Christopher Robin, becomes a central figure in the stories. The other characters are animals. The most important is a teddy bear called Winnie-the-Pooh. The stories are not arranged in a single plot but are independent, as they would be if told by a parent one at a time. Additional stories about the same characters are found in *The House at Pooh Corner*.

Christopher Robin. This character is a young boy who loves his toy animals. The animal characters see him as their superior and come to him with their problems. But, since he is very young, he has limited knowledge. For instance, he wants to go to the North Pole but does not know where or what the North Pole is.

Winnie-the-Pooh. Winnie-the-Pooh loves food, especially honey (spelled "hunny"). He knows that he is a "Bear of Very Little Brain" and shows it by confusing left and right and by not spelling and reading well—or at all. He has enough imagination to use an umbrella as a boat, and he is generous, letting his friend Piglet share his house.

Piglet. Tiny Piglet is Pooh's best friend. His size makes him ready to run from a hint of danger, so he feels ashamed. He overcomes his timidity in a crisis, though. He is a hero when Owl's house collapses. Piglet is thoughtful toward others. For example, he picks flowers for Eeyore the donkey.

Eeyore. The old donkey Eeyore is usually gloomy, predicting bad outcomes for all situations and insisting that everyone dislikes and disrespects him. He allows himself occasional moments of happiness, as

Author's Anecdote

A. A. Milne, the author of *Winnie-the-Pooh*, based many of his animal characters on his son's stuffed animals. For example, the teddy bear on which Pooh is modeled was a gift to the little boy on his first birthday. It is still available for visitors to see at a public library in New York City. Owl and Rabbit, however, were based on real animals that lived in the area of the Milne family farm.

when he plays with his birthday gifts. Eeyore can be considerate toward friends. For example, he finds a home for Owl after Owl's house is wrecked.

Owl. Pompous Owl pretends to be wiser than he really is. He uses big words to sound educated but tends to use them incorrectly.

Rabbit. Rabbit is brighter than the other animals and knows it. He tries to boss others around and to control them with schemes that generally fail.

Tigger. Tigger is a very immature tiger kitten, full of energy that he cannot control. His impulsiveness can lead to accidents. For example, one time he startles Eeyore and makes him fall into a river.

Kanga. Kanga is a mother kangaroo who is apt to smother her baby, Roo, with too much care. She can be harsh with some animals, as she is with Piglet, forcing him to take nasty-tasting medicine when he misbehaves. Toward the immature Tigger, though, she is kind, realizing that he needs mothering.

The Witch of Blackbird Pond ❖ Elizabeth George Speare, 1958, historical/period fiction, Newbery Medal. In 1687, Kit Tyler leaves the island of Barbados to live with the Wood family in a Puritan community in colonial Connecticut. She finds the Wood family's oppressive, rigid way of life burdensome. When she befriends Hannah Tupper, a Quaker woman widely regarded as a heretic, the tension between Kit and the local citizenry grows worse.

Kit Tyler. This character, now 16, grew up in luxury in Barbados. Accustomed to speaking her mind, she now has trouble adapting to a community that views luxury and high spirits negatively; her hot temper also creates problems. She strives to develop more self-control and tolerance.

Matthew Wood. The head of the Wood family is industrious, cheerless, and, after the death of two sons, bitter. He believes that life should be devoted to hard work and prayer.

Rachel Wood. The hard life led by Matthew's wife has left her prematurely aged and tired.

Hannah Tupper. Hannah's Quaker beliefs make her an outcast. The rest of the townsfolk treat Hannah with hostility and suspicion. Despite that treatment, she retains a gentle and loving spirit, giving Kit the benefit of her knowledge. [*See also* THE SIGN OF THE BEAVER by Elizabeth George Speare.]

The Wolves of Willoughby Chase ❖ Joan Aiken, 1962, historical/period fiction. When Sir Willoughby Green takes his wife on a voyage, his daughter, Bonnie, and Bonnie's cousin, Sylvia, remain

Other Works by Joan Aiken

Black Hearts in Battersea
Cold Shoulder Road
The Cuckoo Tree
Dangerous Games
Dido and Pa
Fit of Shivers
Is Underground
Nightbirds on Nantucket
Shadows and Moonshine
The Stolen Lake
The Whispering Mountain

behind with a governess. The governess, Letitia Slighcarp, concocts an evil scheme to get possession of the family estate, Willoughby Chase. The girls try to escape her clutches and protect Sir Willoughby's property until his return.

Bonnie Green. Bonnie is an athletic, spirited girl with a strong moral sense. She is willing to stand up to villains. Bonnie is also a loyal and caring friend, but her impulsiveness (acting without thinking) can lead to trouble.

Sylvia Green. Sylvia, an orphan, is usually well-behaved and obedient. Her thoughtfulness sometimes keeps Bonnie from following risky impulses. Sylvia's quick wits and sharp powers of observation make her a valuable ally.

Letitia Slighcarp. Miss Slighcarp is truly evil. She bullies children and whomever else she can dominate.

Mrs. Gertrude Brisket. This character heads a school for orphans, where Miss Slighcarp plans to place Bonnie and Sylvia after Bonnie's parents are dead. Mrs. Brisket is a taskmaster who abuses the children in her care and makes them work for wages that she keeps for herself.

The Wonderful Wizard of Oz

❖ L. Frank Baum, 1900, fantasy/science fiction/imaginative fiction. Dorothy lives on a Kansas farm with her uncle, her aunt, and her dog Toto, until a cyclone blows the farmhouse—with Dorothy and Toto inside—to the magical Land of Oz. When the house lands on and kills the wicked Witch of the East, Dorothy gets credit for freeing the Munchkins, local inhabitants who had been the witch's unhappy subjects.

Looking for a way back to Kansas, Dorothy heads for the Emerald City, home of the powerful Wizard of Oz. She believes that he can help her. On the road, she gathers an odd assortment of companions: the Scarecrow, the Tin Woodman, and the Cowardly Lion. The three decide to join her in hopes that the Wizard can help them as well. The author also wrote other books about Oz.

Dorothy. Dorothy sees herself as "ordinary," although the Munchkins think she is a witch. She is a considerate girl who wants to help others. She is also brave; for example, she defends Toto against the Cowardly Lion's attack, risking her own life. Though she endures hardships during her quest, she remains determined to reach her goal.

The Scarecrow. This character, with his straw-stuffed body and head, has a low opinion of himself because he lacks a brain. He hopes the Wizard can provide one for him. He is actually intelligent enough to get his friends to build a bridge so that they can escape the Kalidahs.

The Tin Woodman. The Tin Woodman was once flesh and blood, but suffers from a curse placed on him by the wicked Witch of the East. A brave and powerful fighter, he wants the Wizard to give him a heart so that he can be happy. Even in his "heartless" state, he is sweet.

The Cowardly Lion. The Lion believes that he is a coward because he often feels fear. He would like the Wizard to grant him courage. However, all by himself, the Lion overcomes his fear and acts heroically.

The Wizard. Although the inhabitants of Oz believe him to be a powerful wizard, he is only an elderly former circus balloonist who was blown to Oz accidentally. He has used stage and circus trickery—not magical powers—to maintain his reputation in Oz. He is perceptive enough to help the Scarecrow, Tin Woodman, and Cowardly Lion to overcome their lack of confidence, which has been the true source of their unhappiness.

Dorothy and the Scarecrow meet the Tin Man.

A Wrinkle in Time ❖ Madeleine L'Engle, 1962, fantasy/science fiction/imaginative fiction, Newbery Medal. Meg and Charles Wallace Murry are the children of two research scientists. Their father, Mr. Murry, is a specialist in outer-space investigation who vanished without a trace a year ago while in the middle of a project. Since then, Meg, Charles Wallace, and Meg's friend Calvin have become friendly with an eccentric neighbor woman, Mrs. Whatsit. One day, Mrs. Whatsit introduces the three to her equally odd associates, Mrs. Who and Mrs. Which. The three women agree to help the children find Mr. Murry. However, the women warn, this will be no ordinary rescue; the children will have to travel through space and time.

Meg Murry. Twelve-year-old Meg is very intelligent. Her father's absence troubles her greatly, but she takes comfort in the close bond she has with Charles Wallace. Meg finds Mrs. Whatsit and her companions fascinating, and the possibility of locating her father makes her both excited and fearful. During her bizarre adventures, Meg learns that she has more courage and competence than she had thought.

Charles Wallace Murry. Charles Wallace is a brilliant five-year-old with psychic power. Because he rarely talks, people who do not know him well think that he is "slow." Charles has an instinctive grasp of Meg's feelings and thoughts. He cares for her as deeply as she does for him, even though he does not reveal his feelings. In fact, the bond between brother and sister proves essential in their quest.

Calvin O'Keefe. Fourteen-year-old Calvin is Meg's school friend. Tall and thin, Calvin is untidy in appearance and, while he is quite bright, believes himself to be even smarter than he is.

Mrs. Murry. The children's mother is a beautiful woman and brilliant scientist, who has encouraged her children to develop as independent individuals.

Mr. Murry. The children's father is, like their mother, a brilliant scientist. His time in space leaves him changed, as though he were stranded on a desert island.

Mrs. Whatsit. She looks like a delicate storybook grandmother with her wrinkled face, but Mrs. Whatsit actually has great powers.

Mrs. Who. This character wears huge eyeglasses and is fluent in many languages. Her manner of speech is unconventional, and she is fond of making baffling comments.

Mrs. Which. It is not so much what Mrs. Which says as how she sounds that is bizarre; her voice has an echoey quality.

Yang the Youngest and His Terrible Ear ❖

Lensey Namioka, 1992, contemporary realistic fiction. The Yang family, recently arrived in the United States from China, are all talented musicians—except Yingtao, called Fourth Brother by the family. He is an awful violinist because, as musicians say, he has a "terrible ear" for music. His new friend, Matthew Conner, plays the violin well, but Matthew's enthusiasm for music makes his father, Mr. Conner, unhappy. The author has written several books about the Yangs.

Yingtao Yang (Fourth Brother). The Yang family think Yingtao's lack of musical talent is the result of idleness. This charge hurts Yingtao deeply. His natural athletic gifts make him excellent at his newest enthusiasm: baseball.

Matthew Conner. Matthew's love of music helps create a bond between him and Yingtao. Matthew helps his friend Yang learn about baseball and other aspects of American customs, while Matthew picks up knowledge of Chinese culture.

Mr. Yang. This character is a fine musician and teacher. He is rigid in his views, however. For example, he refuses to believe that his son actually does not have an ear for music. Also, he cannot accept the idea of his children taking part-time jobs.

The Yearling ❖

Marjorie Kinnan Rawlings, 1938, historical/period fiction, Pulitzer Prize. This famous novel tells the story of Jody Baxter and his parents. They are a poor backwoods family struggling for survival on a small farm in northern Florida in the years following the Civil War. During the course of the novel, Jody and his father track and kill a bear, Jody's father is bitten by a rattlesnake, and Jody's best friend dies. The main plot revolves around Jody and an orphaned fawn he finds and raises as a pet. The fawn, which Jody names Flag, becomes the center of the boy's life.

In *The Yearling*, Flag, a fawn, becomes the center of Jody Baxter's life.

Jody Baxter. Jody is, in many ways, a typical 12-year-old. He loves to play and always enjoys a joke. But he is different from most boys his age today. There is no school for him to go to, he rarely sees children his own age, and he works all day on the small family farm without complaining. Jody is also unusually serious and sensitive. He thinks a great deal about nature and animals, and, while he loves hunting with his beloved "Pa," he hates the thought that humans must kill in order to eat. Jody's isolated life makes him lonely. He is ecstatic when his parents agree to let him keep Flag, and he loves the fawn deeply. In the end, Jody has to deal with profound loss.

Penny Baxter ("Pa"). Jody's father is a hard-working man who has known much hardship in his life. He is also a gentle, understanding father, who remembers what it was like to be a boy and knows how soon his son will have to give up childhood to become a man. Penny sometimes works harder himself so that Jody can have some time to dream or to go "ramblin'." Honest, strong, and wise, Penny provides the role model that will help Jody to triumph over tragedy.

Year of Impossible Goodbyes ❖ Sook Nyul Choi, 1991, contemporary realistic fiction, ALA Notable Children's Book, ALA

Author's Anecdote

Sook Nyul Choi, the author of *Year of Impossible Goodbyes*, was born in Korea. During the early 1950s, she experienced the horrors of the Korean War, which took place after Korea was divided into North and South Korea. Later, she moved to the United States, where she went to school and remained. Like Sookan in the book, Sook Nyul Choi takes pride in her heritage. One of her goals is to educate readers about Korea's culture and history.

Best Book for Young Adults. This book takes place in Korea late in World War II, when Japan's defeat in the war has ended Japanese rule over Korea. The Korean girl Sookan and her family, who endured great suffering under the Japanese, hope for better times now. However, their northern part of Korea falls under Soviet Russian control, and Communist rulers replace the Japanese. Sookan and her family must try to reach South Korea.

Sookan. This character is ten when the book begins and looks even younger. The harsh conditions of her life force her to grow up quickly. She is proud of her Korean culture and has kept that pride despite constant threats from the Japanese, who consider the Koreans an inferior people. She resists propaganda aimed at getting North Koreans to accept Communist rule in their country.

Inchun. Sookan's little brother, Inchun, is too young to understand the reasons behind the hardship in his life. Often he winds up crying, even when the noise endangers him and Sookan as they try to reach South Korea. At times he shows resilience and strength, and he urges his sister to be brave.

Young Fu of the Upper Yangtze ❖ Elizabeth Foreman Lewis, 1932, historical/period fiction, Newbery Medal.

In early twentieth-century China, **Young Fu,** an ambitious, intelligent boy of 13, and his mother, **Fu Be Be,** move from the country to the city of Chungking. The boy becomes an apprentice to **Tang,** a skilled coppersmith. Young Fu also gets to know an elderly scholar, **Wang,** who tutors the boy in writing. Young Fu learns his craft and lessons about a grown-up's responsibilities.

Zeely ❖ Virginia Hamilton, 1967, contemporary realistic fiction, ALA Notable Children's Book.

Elizabeth Perry and her younger brother, John, spend a summer on their Uncle

Ross's farm. Elizabeth is unprepared for her most fascinating discovery of the summer: a beautiful, tall young woman named Zeely Tayber, who Elizabeth suspects is actually a queen.

Elizabeth Perry. Elizabeth has a vivid imagination and prefers her own company in order to more easily live in a dream world. She makes up fantasies about people and places around her, as well as nicknames. Elizabeth feels a special tie to Zeely, who seems to belong to a magical world.

Zeely Taybcr. Zeely is a young woman of striking appearance. She is six foot six and likes dramatic clothing that emphasizes her unusual looks. She has a special affinity for animals. Zeely senses a connection with Elizabeth, who, like herself, is creative and has a powerful will. [*See also* THE HOUSE OF DIES DREAR and M.C. HIGGINS THE GREAT by Virginia Hamilton.]

Selected Bibliography

Annotated Bibliographies

Apseloff, Marilyn Fain, compiler. *They Wrote for Children Too: An Annotated Biliography of Children's Literature by Famous Writers for Adults.* Westport, CT: Greenwood, 1989.

Children's Books: Awards and Prizes. New York: Children's Book Council, 1996.

Donavin, Denise Perry, editor. *American Library Association's Best of the Best for Children.* New York: Random House, 1992.

Elleman, Barbara, editor. *Children's Books of International Interest.* Chicago: American Library Association, 1984.

Greeson, Janet, and Karen Taha. *Name That Book! Questions and Answers on Outstanding Children's Books.* Metuchen, NJ: Scarecrow, 1986.

Helbig, Alethea K., and Agnes Regan Perkins. *Dictionary of American Children's Fiction: Books of Recognized Merit.* Four volumes. Westport, CT: Greenwood, 1985, 1986, 1993, 1996.

Jones, Dolores Blythe. *Children's Literature Awards and Winners: A Directory of Prizes, Authors, and Illustrators.* Detroit: Gale, 1988.

Larrick, Nancy. *A Parent's Guide to Children's Reading.* New York: Bantam, 1975.

Rand, Donna, Toni Trent Parker, and Sheila Foster. *Black Books Galore! Guide to Great African American Children's Books.* New York: Wiley, 1998.

Stott, Jon C. *Native Americans in Children's Literature.* Phoenix: Oryx, 1995.

Toussaint, Pamela. *Great Books for African-American Children.* New York: Penguin Putnam, 1999.

Weiss, Jaqueline. *Prizewinning Books for Children: Themes and Stereotypes in U.S. Prizewinning Prose Fiction for Children.* Lexington, MA: Heath, 1983.

Anthologies

Arbuthnot, May Hill. *The Arbuthnot Anthology of Children's Literature*, 4th ed. Revised by Zena Sutherland. New York: Lothrop, Lee & Shepard, 1974.

McTigue, Bernard, compiler. *A Children's Garden of Delights: Pictures, Poems, and Stories for Children from the Collections of the New York Public Library.* New York: Abrams, 1987.

Preiss, Byron. *The Best Children's Books in the World: A Treasury of Illustrated Stories.* New York: Abrams, 1996.

Schulman, Janet, and Simon Boughton, editors. *The 20th-Century Children's Book Treasury: Picture Books and Stories to Read Aloud.* New York: Knopf, 1998.

Sutherland, Zena, and Myra Cohn Livingston: *The Scott, Foresman Anthology of Children's Literature.* Glenview, IL: Scott Foresman, 1984.

Books about Children's Literature

Avery, Gillian. *Behold the Child: American Children and Their Books 1621–1922.* Baltimore: Johns Hopkins University Press, 1994.

Bator, Robert. *Signposts to Criticism of Children's Literature.* Chicago: American Library Association, 1983.

Berger, Laura Stanley. *Twentieth-Century Children's Writers*, 4th ed. Detroit: St. James, 1995.

Bloom, Harold, editor. *Women Writers of Children's Literature.* Philadelphia: Chelsea House, 1998.

Carpenter, Humphrey. *Secret Gardens: The Golden Age of Children's Literature from Alice in Wonderland to Winnie-the-Pooh.* Boston: Houghton Mifflin, 1985.

Deane, Paul. *Mirrors of American Culture: Children's Fiction Series in the Twentieth Century.* Metuchen, NJ: Scarecrow, 1991.

Dictionary of Literary Biography, Volume 52: American Writers for Children since 1960: Fiction. Detroit: Gale, 1986.

Egoff, Sheila A. *Thursday's Child: Trends and Patterns in Contemporary Children's Literature.* Chicago: American Library Association, 1981.

Fisher, Margery. *The Bright Face of Danger: An Exploration of the Adventure Story.* Boston: Horn Book, 1986.

Gillespie, John T. *Best Books for Children: Preschool through Grade 6.* Westport, CT: Greenwood, 1998.

Gose, Elliott. *Mere Creatures: A Study of Modern Fantasy Tales for Children.* Toronto: University of Toronto Press, 1988.

Hopkins, Lee Bennett. *The Best of Book Bonanza.* New York: Holt, Rinehart & Winston, 1980.

Hunt, Peter. *International Companion Encyclopedia of Children's Literature.* London: Routledge, 1996.

Kohn, Herbert. *Should We Burn Babar? Essays on Children's Literature and the Power of Stories.* New York: New Press, 1995.

L'Engle, Madeleine, and Avery Brooke. *Trailing Clouds of Glory: Spiritual Values in Children's Books.* Philadelphia: Westminster, 1985.

Lipson, Eden Ross. *The New York Times Parent's Guide to the Best Books for Children.* New York: Three Rivers Press, 2000.

Lysted, Mary. *From Dr. Mather to Dr. Seuss: 200 Years of American Books for Children.* Boston: Hall, 1980.

McCann, Donnarae, and Gloria Woodard, editors. *The Black American in Books for Children: Readings in Racism,* 2d ed. Metuchen, NJ: Scarecrow, 1985.

McClure, Amy A., and Jancie V. Kristo, editors. *Books That Invite Talk, Wonder, and Play.* Urbana, IL: National Council of Teachers of English, 1966.

Moynihan, William T., and Mary E. Shaner. *Masterworks of Children's Literature: The Twentieth Century.* New York: Chelsea House, 1986.

Nodelman, Perry, editor. *Touchstone: Reflections on the Best in Children's Literature.* Two volumes. West Lafayette, IN: Children's Literature Association, 1985, 1987.

Pfeffer, Susan Beth. *Who Were They Really? The True Stories behind Famous Characters.* Brookfield, CT: Millbrook, 1999.

Pflieger, Pat. *A Reference Guide to Modern Fantasy for Children.* Westport, CT: Greenwood, 1984.

Rees, David. *Painted Desert, Green Shade: Essays on Contemporary Writers of Fiction for Children and Young Adults.* Boston: Horn Book, 1984.

———. *What Do Draculas Do? Essays on Contemporary Writers of Fiction for Children and Young Adults.* Metuchen, NJ: Scarecrow, 1990.

Stott, Jon C. *Children's Literature from A to Z: Guide for Parents and Teachers.* New York: McGraw-Hill, 1984.

Sutton, Wendy K. *Adventuring with Books: A Booklist for Pre-K–Grade 6.* Champaign, IL: National Council of Teachers of English, 1993.

Townsend, John Rowe. *Written for Children (25th Anniversary Edition): An Outline of English-Language Children's Literature.* New York: HarperCollins, 1990.

(continued from page ii)

Index

Page numbers for features about authors are in boldface type. Page numbers for illustrations are in italics. Characters are listed under their first name or polite title (e.g., *Aunt*). For characters whose names are also book titles, look in the A–Z section by book title.